Tell Your Story Walking

One Mother's Legacy

Iris Llewellyn Angle

INFINITY PUBLISHING

Copyright © 2011 by Iris Llewellyn Angle

ISBN 978-0-7414-7027-0

Printed in the United States of America

Published October 2012

INFINITY PUBLISHING
1094 New DeHaven Street, Suite 100
West Conshohocken, PA 19428-2713
Toll-free (877) BUY BOOK
Local Phone (610) 941-9999
Fax (610) 941-9959
Info@buybooksontheweb.com
www.buybooksontheweb.com

**In Memory
of
Eric Michael Llewellyn**

**Dedicated
To
My husband Jim,
My daughter Laura,
And to all those who
Grieve, Survive, and Thrive.**

This is my story and the people in it are real. I used the real names of all my family, friends, and people who inspired and impacted my life. However, I did change the names of some of the people I met on my physical pilgrimage to protect their privacy and their stories.

Contents

Prologue

I spread my hand woven Mexican blanket next to a flat, black granite stone that reads:

Eric Michael Llewellyn
November 21, 1972 - January 7, 1993
He gave us love and laughter

Between the dates, a bicycle balances on its back wheel ready to zoom away. I kneel and pull weeds that strangle the drooping daffodils. I touch a red rock from Arizona I put here last summer. I write my son a letter asking for help on how to begin his story. I sit and wait.

When Eric whispers, I begin to write. "Begin with the dream of me coming to tell you a story that you would not listen to. Listen now. Begin with that dream, the one you will never forget. Share your healing process, which is also mine. I had to die to heal: yes, write that. I had to die to heal.

Tell your story of healing and you will tell mine. I watch over you, and your healing journey heals me in every step you take. You give me strength, too, with your prayers, with the love letters you are writing in your journal, and with your poems. Every time you share our story with someone who has thought about suicide, or with someone who has lost a loved one to suicide, I am with you. You chose this healing journey, which continues to heal us both. Tell that story."

Eric's voice strengthens. "You are ready to hear the story I came to tell you in that dream. In the story a boy is afraid to become a man. He feels like a loser yet doesn't want to let anyone down, especially his mother. He is torn.

He hurts so much he wants only to end his pain. He doesn't want to die. He just doesn't know what else to do.

"Tell how his action forces you to choose to live. Tell how that living helps the boy and his mother to heal. Tell our story."

Journal Entry
April 29, 1994

I couldn't sleep last night. The events of the day replayed in my mind. What is wrong with me? I thought if I did everything right during that first nightmare year after Eric's death, I would feel better this second year. But no, I'm more depressed and hopeless than ever. Yes, I survived Eric's 21st birthday without him, then Christmas Day, a year to the day I last saw him. I didn't know how I would make it through January 7th, the anniversary of his death. And the anniversary of his funeral, which this year was just as dark, cold, and gloomy as the day they lowered his body into the snow-covered ground. Shouldn't I be feeling better? What is wrong with me? I can't do anything right. I don't feel like doing anything, not even reading, which I love, or walking. I want only to stay in bed and never get up. I feel so worthless, a nobody, a failure.

Then I had THE dream. Throughout his life, seeing our bedroom light on, Eric often knocked on our door and asked to come in. He would tell Jim and me a funny story, a joke, or something about his day. In the dream, he came into our room and started to tell me a story. I did not listen to him. I wanted what I wanted: to look at him, to touch him. He left. Was it to punish me for not listening? Before he disappeared, I felt his arms around me, just for a moment. So real a feeling, I thought Kitty, our sixty-pound, Collie had jumped on me. It wasn't Kitty though. I knew my son had given me one last hug.

This dream-gift from Eric was the beginning of my healing. I woke up smiling and wrote this poem:

This Gift

It was a dream, wasn't it?
You came into my room to tell me a story;
I see your face and hear your voice.
What are you telling me?

You came into my room to tell me a story.
Come back! You have not finished the story.
What are you telling me?

I am not listening, not understanding.
Come back! You have not finished the story.
I know you have to leave me again...
I am not listening, not understanding.
Then my body feels you.

I know you have to leave me again...
I see your face and hear your voice.
Then my whole body feels you.
It was a dream, wasn't it?
This gift.

Part One

Grieving

Chapter One

Hold On

First Things First
Death Year

"First things first" your suicide note said,
"Mom, I love you and you didn't do anything wrong."
Now you are sleeping in the hard white ground,
Instead of performing tricks on your bike,
You decided to die.
Now I must make it through today.

January 7, 1993

I talked to Eric last night. He sounded upbeat and happy. I asked him, "Are you high on something? You sound so different."

"Yes, I'm high on life. I'm excited about my job interview next week."

We talked a few minutes. Then he asked to speak to Jim, his stepfather, an unusual request, I thought.

"Jim, I just wanted to say hi." We chatted about Laura, his sister with whom he had gone to live in Phoenix. He had had lunch with his dad, Bob who also lived there. Hanging up, I said, "Good luck and I love you."

"I love you, too, Mom."

Eric left Ohio on Christmas Day, driving to Phoenix to start again. He had moved to Phoenix last August, but came back in October after celebrating Laura's birthday with her. He didn't know what he wanted to do or where he wanted to live. After a short stay here, he planned to go back to

Phoenix. I talked him into staying until Christmas as Laura would be coming home.

This morning I'm in his room cleaning out a wooden file cabinet that I want to use in my office.

Sorting through bits of paper, I find a letter my brother Ed wrote to him last year after Eric quit high school. Other scraps of stationery are poems old girlfriends had written to him. It's hard not to read them. I find a package of prophylactics. "I'd better send these to you in case you need them," I say and laugh. A yellowish folder is labeled in a child's handwriting: My Journal, Eric Llewellyn, 2nd Grade, Mrs. Jevnikar.

"I like to ride my bike. It is fun. My mom works for an i doctor. She likes it. I like sumr. We went boting. It was fun. I plad futball and sockr and rolr-skate. It was fun. I like to ride my bike. It is fun. I fall a cupll of times but it is still fun." It continues with all the things he did at eight. He went to the circus, to his grandmother's, played with his cousins, watched football, had a birthday party, made a Christmas angel, went sledding many times. "Me and my mom read the black Stallion," he wrote and then every sentence, "It was fun." Many entries were about riding his bike and learning to do tricks on it. I find a picture of Eric at fourteen and remember the day it was taken.

I was cleaning up the kitchen for the third time and heard Eric yell from the yard. Not an I'm-hurt-come-help-me yell, but a come-quick-I-want-to-show-you-something yell. I ran out the family-room door to the front yard and looked up and down the driveway. No Eric. I strolled around to the backyard, still no Eric. Where is he?

"Up here, Mom, up here!"

I looked up to see Eric and his friend Mark standing on the peak of the garage roof, grinning. Mark was waving one hand while the other held the front of Eric's bike. Eric was holding the back wheel. I can see their giant grins from the ground.

"How in the world did you boys get up there and how did you get the bike up there?" I wailed. "And get down from there, right this minute!"

They never did tell me how they did it. But the next picture gives me an idea: bare trees, snow-covered ground, the edge of the garage, and a flying bicycle!

I think, "Oh, Eric, I hope you have fun in Phoenix. I hope you find what you're looking for."

Christmas 1992 was the happiest I'd ever experienced. My kids were home, and Jim's daughter had recently given us our first grandchild, Jimmy, at six -months old made Christmas fun. A fitting mood to go into a year of new beginnings as a new college graduate, a businesswoman, a woman on the move to where I can only wonder.

"Honey, I'm home," I hear Jim call. "Scott's right behind me."

"I'll be down in a minute." I forgot we were taking Jim's son to dinner.

I had achieved my goal of organizing my office. Time for dinner and a visit with Scott, a relaxing evening.

I hear Kitty barking.

Coming downstairs, I see a policeman in the living room talking to Jim.

"Are you Iris Llewellyn Angle's husband? Is she home?"

"Yes, yes."

When I came into the living room, the policeman said, "Please have a seat." I struggled to hear him as he spoke softly.

"Last night about four in the morning, your son drove into the desert just south of Phoenix, smoked two cigarettes, wrote a note, and shot himself."

What was he saying? It couldn't be Eric; he didn't smoke, didn't own a gun. "I need to call him to make sure he's all right." Someone screamed and then the room was silent.

I don't remember the policeman or Scott leaving. I do remember Jim saying, "We need to call and tell Laura."

"But she's there, she must already know!"

"No, honey. They identified Eric from his Ohio driver's license. They didn't know he moved to Phoenix."

I could not tell her. Jim had to do it. She screamed so loud, I could hear it through the phone line.

Jim told her, "You have to tell your dad."

After that call, my memory disappeared along with my strength. All I had was silence.

> So many words swimming in my head.
> So many words need to be said.
> Can't say it.
> Must say it.
> Just say it.
> He's dead.
> My son is dead.

Our house was full of people that night, but who? I remember tears and laughter, telling story after story about Eric, then silence. What does someone say to a mother whose son just killed himself?

My body went on automatic pilot and my mind someplace else, a place it had never been before. Would it ever come back? Some senses dulled. I could not hear. I could not taste food. I could not speak. Some senses heightened. I could smell Eric's Polo cologne. I could see Eric alone in the desert. I could feel his presence.

Where were we driving to? A funeral home to make arrangements. For whom? I did not want the answer, so I named the objects in the car: door, window, handle, seat, seatbelt, floor, ceiling. The names kept me from thinking about my son lying out in the desert, alone and dead.

Nan, an old friend, and her husband Mark own the funeral home we chose. I saw the shocked look on Nan's face before they began asking questions. What kind of casket do you want? Where will the service be held? What day and time? Where will he be buried? When will his body arrive? Will the casket be opened or closed?

My mind disappears again. I begin naming the objects in the room; chair, desk, rug, lamp, table, curtains, wall, ceiling. They're closing in on me. Am I going crazy? How will I survive this? Eric, why did you choose to leave me? Didn't you love me enough to stay? Why didn't you love yourself enough to live? The question why, why, why? How long will I ask why? Will I ever find the answer? And who do I ask?

I'll start with Eric.

January 23, 1993

Dear Eric,

I'm exhausted from crying, yet I don't know what else to do. Christmas Day when I said goodbye to you, I didn't cry because I knew I would be visiting you in February when I visit Laura as I've done since she moved there.

On New Year's Eve, you called us collect at our friends, Roger and Carol. Accepting the charges, they laughed, happy to hear your voice and we all wished each other a Happy New Year.

I was excited for you, starting a new year in Phoenix with your sister and dad. You sounded excited.

When you called six days later on the night before you died, I said, "I love you."

You said, "I love you too, Mom." You didn't say it often, but I knew you loved me. But not enough to live, not enough to tell me you were hurting, that's why I'm so confused. And not enough to change your life. How much would have been enough? I would have loved to help you by talking it out.

To use the first sentence in your suicide note, "First things first, I love you, and you didn't do anything wrong." You underlined it four times. Were you thinking of me when you wrote that, knowing I would blame myself for your decision? I do blame myself. I am your mother. I should have known you were in pain. Why didn't I see it?

Why didn't you tell me or tell someone else, anyone? How can I think that I didn't do anything wrong when you chose to die, throwing away the life I gave you? At this moment, I feel that you did something terribly wrong, and I don't understand your reasons.

Will I ever understand them? I wonder if in the second after you pulled the trigger, you felt you'd made a mistake. You often made quick decisions, acted on them without considering the consequences, then realized you made a mistake and corrected it. Remember the time you quit school and then realized it was a mistake and went back? I was so proud of you.

But this time you can't go back.

Then your note said, "I'm just a loser, and nothing could have changed that. What can I say besides I had nothing to live for." Where did those thoughts come from? I know you were having a difficult time figuring out how you fit in this world. You saw your friends going to college, getting jobs, enjoying life while you didn't know what you wanted to do or even where you wanted to live. But you didn't give yourself a chance to get through this difficult time. You didn't give me a chance to help you. You didn't wait for me to catch up to you—and to catch on.

And now you're dead.

I still cannot comprehend that statement. I will never see your face again. I will never see the ladder standing against your balcony for you to sneak back into your room because you forgot your key. I will never see you changing the oil in your car or hear you tell a funny joke. I will never watch another movie with you. How will I live without you?

Where are you? I hope you are at peace. I believe that if you had looked ahead to imagine the pain it would cause, you would never have taken your life. I had no idea that you were in such pain. I wish you had told someone, anyone and that they had come to me, you might still be here today.

I thank God your last words were, "I love you." I wish I could have helped you more, helped you find someone to help you realize that you were never a loser and had much to live for. I know you went to some friends, but many of them may have had similarly dark thoughts and feelings.

Eric, I pray that the choice to end your life will have an impact on them keeping them from making the same decision. I sense my life's work will be to help others not make the choice to die. But how can I do that when I can't even breathe or move or write?

I love you. Mom

P.S. I found several poems in the box of notes and letters you kept. I don't know who wrote "Not For Long." I wonder how you responded to it.

Not For Long

I've let you go
but not for long.
You made my heart sing
a new kind of song.
I cannot let you do
what you want to do,
after all we've been through.
You have the dearest place
in my heart. I wanted to make
us closer, to make you love me
more. You know what you
have done. Has the time come
to try again?

9

How long will it take for me not to cry every day? How long will it take for me to live fully again? How long?

It took me a while but I finally wrote to his friends, thanking them for being pallbearers: Gabe, Rob, Jamie, Ryan, Mark, Ben, Brad, Matt. What was going through their minds as they carried that box with Eric's body across the frozen snow? And what would he have thought if he had seen their faces, looking as if they had lost their way and would never find it again. I shouldn't have to be writing these letters; his friends shouldn't have to receive them. But I have to give them encouragement, give them the help I couldn't give Eric:

"You were all special to Eric, and I know he was special to you. I believe that if he had known how much you cared for and loved him, he would be here today. I want to share with you some words that are comforting me in hopes that they will comfort you. In his death, Eric is giving us a gift he could not give in his life. The gift to help us realize how important we all are to the people in our lives, to live life to the fullest, to love and cherish the people we love and tell them so. To use our talents, skills, and interests to make a difference in our lives and in our world.

I have chosen to keep Eric's memory alive by using my speaking talents to speak to schools, churches, community groups, and anyone else who needs to hear Eric's story. I want to prevent others from making the same decision Eric made. I want to tell them that there are people who want to help if we give them the chance. If I can prevent one person from making that final choice, I will consider my life a success. I know your lives have changed because of Eric's death. I pray that you will find your unique way to keep Eric's memory alive. Thank you for being his friend."

I feel like a different person since Eric died. Some days are okay, and some days I can't stop crying. I miss him more than I could ever imagine. It feels strange, so unreal, when I say to people, "My son died." When they ask how, I respond, "By his own hand."

I want to learn about suicide and depression. I want to help people who are hurting but don't know where to turn. I want to stop people from making that final decision, to prevent people like me from feeling this pain. Did he have any idea? No, of course not. If he had, I don't think he would have done what he did. I wish he had talked to someone, to anyone who might have helped. I wish I had known about Eric's pain. Did he plan it, or was it an impulsive act? I wish I knew. I wish, I wish, I wish.

April 7, 1993

Dear Eric,

These letters to you help both Laura and me. I found out she talks to you, too. Thanks for sending her the sign that you wanted her to have your car. After driving her scooter 30 miles to work every day, it was ready to die. Last month on her way to work she thought about your car and how she could use it. She yelled over the traffic, "Please Eric, send me a sign, do you want me to have your car?" A mile down the road, her scooter stopped running. You answered her.

Maybe that's why you got out of your car before using the gun. She found a bullet on the floor and cried. I'm glad she found a Survivor of Suicide group to attend. I hope it helps her. I need to find one, too.

I've been collecting poems and found this comforting one from The Prophet, *by* Kahil Gibran:

> Only when you drink from the river of silence shall you indeed sing.

And when you have reached the mountaintop, then you shall begin to climb.
And when the earth shall claim your limbs, then shall you truly dance.

I hope you are dancing now. You didn't do much dancing in your life, except the time you got up and did the hula with the hula dancer at a Luau at the apartment where you stayed with your dad last year. I still laugh when I watch the video. It shows the muscles in your arms and a manly chest. That's the Eric I want to remember. In all your baby and school pictures, you smiled and acted goofy. When did you stop smiling, and why didn't I notice?

You didn't sing or smile much in the last few years. Were you in that much pain? All I am left with is to ask, wonder, think, change, and learn to live again.

Do you miss me, Laura, your dad, your step-dad, and your friends?

We all miss you. I love you and miss you. Mom

P.S. I did experience joy since you died. You remember my friend Shannon? She had a baby girl, Amber, the week before you died and she could not drive up from Cincinnati for your funeral. But a month later, she packed Amber into the car and came north to visit me. She needed to see me and wanted me to meet her new little girl. Shannon placed Amber in my arms where she stayed the entire weekend. I cried as I first held her.

Shannon and I talked about that night. When she answered the phone on January 7th, she sounded sleepy and annoyed. "Who is this?" She hadn't recognized my voice. "It's after 11:00 and I just had a baby. I'm exhausted."

Whatever I answered, she knew something was wrong. I said, "Eric is dead. I had to call you." I tried to explain what happened but couldn't. After hanging up, she said she lay in her husband's arms and cried the rest of the night. Then I cried as I held her new baby in my arms.

Shannon called a couple of days after returning home from our visit. She wanted to ask us a question. "Iris would Jim and you be Amber's godparents?" Without hesitation or discussion, we said yes!

Chapter Two

The Desert

June 7, 1993

Dear Eric,

I need to write to you today, five months since you made the decision to end your life. I still have a difficult time with that thought. Sometimes I think it never happened I think you're on a long trip and can't call me.

When I walked today, I thought about the last day I saw you, Christmas Day. I can't think about this Christmas to come, I have to get past your birthday. I think of you, say your name, and cry. How long will this go on?

I don't think I told you about my visit to Laura in March. We talked and talked about you and your last two weeks with her in Phoenix. Laura is still struggling with the guilt of not being there for you. When you said, "So long," she thought she'd see you the next day.

We went through your few things. What should we keep? What should we give away? I kept your tennis racquet, your answering machine and some of your sweat shirts. Laura took your shirts, ski boots, and odds & ends. We divided up your audio tapes. Maybe someday I'll go through them and find the one you were playing that night in the desert. It felt strange to hold your things. I kept thinking you'd walk through the door any minute and ask, "What are you doing with my underwear?"

I called my friend Dick today and this time he was in his office. I met him in 1985 when he was in Cleveland on business. Every time I came to visit Laura, I'd call him but he was always out of town. I told him about you. He said,

"I'm picking you up in an hour to go to lunch. No argument."

We talked about how we met, his visits to Ohio, about his dad, who died recently and how his mother was doing. We talked about his two daughters and Laura. I told him, "One day I want to find the place where Eric died." The location on your death certificate was given as: Hunt Highway and Lindsay Rd. He knew the place. After lunch we drove south into the desert.

Oh, Eric, how did you end up there? Did you get lost? It's such a desolate road with nothing around for miles but it is peaceful. Did you feel the peace? And did you see the stars? Was Orion looking down on you?

I talked to Deputy Campbell, who found you. Someone had reported hearing a gunshot and he investigated it. He said you were listening to a copy of a tape, not a store-bought one, some kind of rock music. He found it where you were standing outside the car along with two cigarette butts. He found your note on the dashboard. As I stood on the spot where you made your last decision, I tried to feel what you felt, to think what you thought. I cried. I am worn out from crying.

I talked to your Uncle Ed last week. He's having a difficult time. He was so excited when he saw you before Christmas. You told him you'd visit him in Atlanta. He wanted to be a real uncle to you. He's angry at you for not giving him a chance. He's angry at you for giving up. I'm angry at you. People tell me I will get over the anger and I'd like to believe that. I will work on my anger.

I cry every day. How long will this go on? For a moment this morning I could see the hurt and pain on Jim's face. He is angry with you, too. All three of us have much healing to do.

If only I could have seen your pain. If only you could have shared it with someone. If only someone, anyone could have helped you. If only I could have helped you. I must quit saying "if only" and start saying-- oh, I don't know what I want to say.

I found this page on a quote-of-the-day calendar from Thursday, January 7, 1993, the day you died.

There are often events in our lives that just do not make sense. In spite of our best efforts, projects fail. It is important to take stock of the situation, accept our part in the failure, and then move on.

When we get stuck on the "why" we can stay stuck for a long time. We want to understand, and it is so difficult to admit that some things just don't make sense.

Faith in living does not ask why. Faith in living asks how and does it. How long will I stay stuck in why? When will I find the faith to go on living? I think I'll go out into the sunshine and think of you. I love you, Mom.

> The warm sun shines down on me.
> My loving son shines down on me.
> Are you at peace?
> Good-bye for now, my son.

In an essay I wrote for a humanities class at Lakeland Community College just before Eric was born, I wrote, "What Is Death?" based on Walt Whitman's *"Song of Myself."* Whitman believed that when one person dies, another life form begins:

"I bequeath myself to the dirt to grow from the grass I love, if you want me again look for me under your boot-soles."

He is not only in the ground, he is the ground. Another life has begins after the speaker's death. Similarly, his death ceases the moment life appears from the ground. The cycle of life, not just man's, continues to exist in another life form, grass. Whitman is not alarmed by death but saw it as an escape from life. Many agree, seeing death is an escape from pain, misery, sorrow, and defeat; some even feel it is more lucky to die than it is to be born:

"And as to you Life I reckon you are the leavings of many deaths."

Life continues through death and death continues through life:

"It is not chaos or death--it is form, union, plan--it is eternal life--it is Happiness."

Did I really write these words? Did I mean them or did I just want the A- I received and the comment, good treatment? I can't recall but now these are more than empty words in an old essay. Whitman accepts death as a part of life and is clearly at peace with death. Will I ever be at peace with Eric's death?

I ate something today. I did get dressed. I can't remember the last time I talked to anyone but Jim and Laura, but then the phone rang.

"Hi, Iris, it's Cecelia. How are you? Just calling to confirm that you'll be presenting your *Nuts and Bolts of Marketing* seminar next month."

What is she talking about? I had not talked to her since last November, which means she doesn't know about Eric.

"Oh, Cecelia, my son died in January. I have no energy to present a workshop. I can't even stop crying." I told her about how, when, and where Eric died and what these last few months have been like. "I just can't do it, Cecelia."

"Yes, you can, and you need to do it for your healing. You need to do this to move forward, to take a step into the living world. I'll call you every week to see how you're doing, and I'll be with you the night of the seminar. Talk to you next week."

That other life, my life before Eric's death, flashes into my mind. I am a new college graduate starting my own business. I am excited about the future, professionally and personally. I'm finally living the life I've always dreamed of living.

In the spring of 1992 I graduated from Kent State University, achieving my lifelong dream. Between raising two kids, holding down part-time and full-time jobs, and enduring divorce, remarriage, and all the demands of daily life, it only took me twenty-five years, but I did it. For a graduation gift, Jim and I traveled to Germany. My brother and brother-in-law, both in the Army, were stationed there with their families. My brother, sister, and I hadn't been together for ten years because they were always on opposite sides of the world from me. We enjoyed a day together with their kids at the Heidelberg Zoo.

After returning home and doing nothing for a month, it was time to start my business: sales and promotion for small businesses; writing marketing plans; and designing and implementing sales-training programs. I began promoting my business by becoming the director of a small business organization. I was responsible for the monthly newsletter, finding speakers for the monthly meeting, and enlisting new members.

Also to market my business, I developed an introductory marketing seminar that I presented at local community education centers. The one Cecelia called me about had been scheduled last September. I knew the material and had presented it many times last year. But now I didn't have the courage or energy to stand up and speak in front of a group of strangers like I normally would. My heart wasn't in it. My mind was on Eric, on death, depression, pain, and sorrow, not marketing. How could I be normal when there is no normal for me anymore? Who cares about marketing? Besides, the community education center is paying good money for needed information from a professional. I didn't feel like a professional. I felt like a mother whose son had just killed himself.

Every time Cecelia called, I told her I could not do it. The day before the workshop she said, "You don't have to do this for the participants. You do have to do this for yourself. You need to do this to be able to go on with your life—it's one small, beginning step in your healing. They will get the information they need because you will stand there as a professional and do your job. You need to do this for your survival."

I don't remember what I said that night or how many people attended, but I do remember that I did it. Cecelia sat in front, smiling and sending me support. When I finished she gave me a strong hug. I did learn that I can go on living by taking one action, one step and with a friend at my side.

One day my friend Julie called. She said, "I have a friend whose son took his own life a couple of years ago. Would you like to talk to her?"

"Yes, yes, yes!" I replied.

When Eric completed suicide I did not know anyone who had experienced a suicide in their family. Oh, I knew about the self-inflicted deaths of famous people: Marilyn Monroe, Ernest Hemingway, and Sylvia Plath, for example, but no one in my world. I wanted to talk to someone who could reassure me that I wasn't going crazy and that I would survive. I needed someone to talk to who had been down this path. I did meet a couple from my church whose son had killed himself a few months before Eric did, but they were still in heavy grief and couldn't answer my questions, especially as they were still asking that one huge question: Why?

I met Julie's friend for coffee one afternoon. I sat and listened to her, and she listened to me. For the first time I felt someone knew what I had been going through. I don't remember much of the conversation, and she could knock on my door today and I would not recognize her, but what I do remember helped me realize I would survive. When she spoke, her words made sense. I knew how she felt, as I had the same feelings. She was breathing normally, and she even smiled a couple of times. I thought, if she can do it, so can I. But I knew it would take time and effort to work through my grief.

Until I met this real survivor, I thought I was the only person in the world this had happened to, but I've learned differently. Suicide affects more people than we realize. We just don't know about it because no one talks about it. After I started telling people that my son took his own life, I met more and more people who had experienced it but who didn't want to acknowledge it.

A few days later my friend Nancy called to tell me her friend's daughter had completed suicide. "Do you feel strong enough to talk to her?" she asked. "I think you could really help her." What would I say? Maybe I could listen and when I talked, I could make sense, then breathe and even smile a couple of times. That sounded like a plan.

Maybe one of my purposes is to talk to people about suicide. People are uncomfortable when I tell them my son died by suicide but I need to say it. The more I say it, the more real it becomes to me. Sometimes it seems like a nightmare that I'll wake from soon. Then I go to his grave. It is real when I sit there and place my cup of coffee on the corner of his stone. It is real when I read his name, his birth date, and his death date in the hard black stone. It is real when I read the words, "He gave us love and laughter." It's all too real.

> I found the amethyst stone I gave him.
> I placed it on the black stone sinking
> Into the hard ground, the ground where
> He is buried. I planted purple irises to
> Remind him of me. Maybe his decomposed
> Body will help them grow. I brought home

The angel candle to remind me of him.
I do not need anything to remind me.

I'm sitting at Eric's grave, thinking. This is a place I never thought I'd be. This is an experience I never dreamed I'd have. But I'm here often, like a bad habit I can't break. I pull the weeds and dead flowers from around his stone and brush away the dirt. I'm drinking my fifth cup of coffee and using the flat stone as a table. I am with Eric.

I feel stronger, almost like my old carefree self. Is that possible? Someone even mentioned the other day that I'm still crazy. I took it as a compliment.

Summer is over and kids are back in school. Even Laura is taking a class at Mesa Community College. She called yesterday to remind me of the date, nine months to the day since Eric died. Nothing has changed, and yet everything has changed. Tears still come when I say his name. But I have decided to go on living, to live every day to the fullest and to make Eric's life and death mean something. I don't know what or how yet.

I believe God chooses each of us to do something for Him. He has a plan. We just have to listen and follow. Is that what I'm doing? Maybe I should be silent and listen more. I feel that God is preparing me for something, something great. Am I on target with his plan? Am I moving at his pace or mine? I don't know. But I am moving forward.

I know that Eric's life was important to more people than he realized: family and friends and people he didn't even know. I wish he could have known that he was not a loser or a failure but a kid who didn't yet have direction and couldn't yet see the future. If only I had shown him that; if only, if only, if only.

In July we had a memorial picnic. That January day of Eric's funeral was cold and dreary. Six months later it was hot and bright. Friends: Eric's, Laura's, and ours gathered. We felt his presence. I read a poem from *The Prophet* about

21

children not belonging to us and a poem called "Remember Me." Jim and my sister Rosie both read poems. I invited everyone to share their feelings, to tell a story or say whatever they wanted. Gabe started and slowly others followed. I wish I could remember what people said but I was crying and laughing so much. Laura told this story:

"I was so excited about having a baby brother to play with. One morning I jumped into Eric's crib. I wanted him to help me put Mr. Potato Head together. I almost poked Eric's eye out with Mr. Potato Head's ear. I felt so bad."

We laughed and cried as we shared stories about Eric and each said they missed him. I brought my boom box and played the "Prayer" from *Les Miserables* and "Friends" by Michael W. Smith, which we had played at his funeral. Then we went to Chardon Park for a picnic. In all my preparation and excitement, I forgot the hot dogs and hamburgers. An old Chardon neighbor Clay offered to go to the store and ended up cooking them, too. I shared the reasons I wanted to have this celebration.

"I want to give you all an opportunity to speak words you couldn't speak six months ago. I want us to gather as a community of people who loved Eric, miss him, and give him a proper good-bye. I want to give those of you who couldn't come to the funeral in January a memorial service to attend. I want to see all of you to make sure you're doing okay. I want us to think about where we go from here. What do we do now?

"How do we make our lives and Eric's life count for something? What are the gifts he gave us? How can we use our talents to make this world a better place? How can we help others not to make the decision Eric made? I've been asking these questions and searching for the answers. I haven't found them yet. Maybe we can help each other. Thank you, Eric, for giving us this time together. Thank you for your love and laughter."

The sound of a lawnmower in the distance reminds me that life goes on even in a cemetery. One day when I came to visit, a funeral had just ended. I saw two people standing by an open grave. I heard mournful music coming from behind a giant maple tree. A man fingered the tall bagpipes that played "Amazing Grace" as I stood listening, thinking.

Last night after I put my head on my pillow and closed my eyes, I saw Eric at the age of four. He wore a cowboy hat and made funny faces and laughed. I also have a photograph of him wearing a cowboy hat and laughing. So was my dream actually a memory? Some of both? He did laugh often when he was a little boy. I don't know when he stopped laughing. He had a unique sense of humor and loved to make people laugh. He also loved to say and do things to shock people. Is that partly why he killed himself? I will never know for sure.

My tears, raindrops on fallen leaves
That I clear from the black granite stone.
I want to share my mint-chocolate-chip ice cream
With you and give you one last bear hug.
The mockingbird mocks me and a bee buzzes
In my ear reminding me you are not here.
But in the laughing eyes of a four-year-old and
In raindrops on golden leaves, I hear you.

November 21, 1993

Dear Eric,

I made it through the first birthday since you died, your special birthday, 21 on the 21ˢᵗ. I was dreading it and cried two or three times, trying to fill the day with activities, hoping not to think about you so much. I did not succeed.

Jim and I visited your grave. I think your grandparents left you a plant. The pumpkin I left is still there. Someone left a tobacco can, probably Gabe. I found notes from your friends. "Thinking of you Lewy. We all miss you, man. Engleke" and "Too all the good times! The good beers! Your best friend, Matt." We took Gabe and Rob to dinner at your favorite restaurant, Red Lobster, and toasted your birthday. We all wished you were with us. I think of you every day. Especially now, as you were living with us this time last year.

Kelly Services called for you the other day, updating their records. I said, "My son is dead." I am not looking forward to the holidays. I hope you can feel and hear and maybe even see how much I miss you. Happy 21ˢᵗ Birthday, Eric.

Love, Mom

I am growing stronger. I cry only once a day now. I'm thinking about the future and how I fit into this crazy world. I believe I am preparing for some great thing, greater than I ever dreamed I could possibly do. I don't know what it is but I need to prepare. I tell people I'm in training for my big assignment.

They ask, "In training for what?"

"I don't know yet," I say. I'll search, investigate, and train so when it appears, I'll be ready.

Two weeks ago my friend Helen and I attended a *Common Boundary* conference in Washington, D.C. The title, "Nourish the Soul" intrigued us. The *Common Boundary* magazine combines spirituality, psychology, and creativity. Could this combination help me get through these first anniversaries, Eric's birthday, Christmas, the anniversary of his death?

The first workshop I attended was "Creativity as a Spiritual Path" with poet, novelist, and storyteller Deena Metzger. She says that spirituality begins with a question. My question is:

What is my purpose and how do I accomplish it? How do I get from here to there?

Then she asked, "Are you willing to hear and receive the answer to the question?" Yes, I am willing to hear the answer. My purpose is to tell Eric's story. How do I do that? When will I be ready? Start by writing about a recent event. I wrote about the day I presented my Competent Toastmasters speech at the district Toastmasters conference last week. This tenth speech qualifies one as a Competent Toastmaster, a polished and qualified speaker.

I wore my new royal blue suit, a perfect color for my complexion because it makes me look healthy and alive. I feel strong and professional and scared. I have lived this speech for the past year. Strange faces filled the room, but emotionally I was not in this room, I was in my speech. I was fulfilling my mission, to speak about someone choosing to die--not just someone, my son. I take a breath, say a prayer. I tell myself, "I am strong. I have an important message to share." I begin. I do not cry. I see the pain in their eyes. I hear their sighs. I feel their compassion. I tell Eric's story.

Then Deena asked us to write the titles of six books we need to write before we die. I could think of only one: *Rough Road Ahead.*

Deena says that the times of darkness are our times of growth. Through suffering we weave stories that nourish the soul. The more we heal, the more spiritual we become. She said, "Write the first lines of a long poem you cannot finish." I wrote:

Why did you leave me?
Where did you go?
Why didn't you love me enough to stay?
Why didn't you love yourself enough to stay?
You could not...
I could not...

The world is white like that day we
Lowered your body into the hard ground.
Again, I feel the shiver through my body

As I stood watching the circle grow around
Your grave. I feel the hot tears on my face
As I kiss you good-bye. I stand asking why,
Why did you choose to die?
A question I continue to ask.

December 23, 1993
Dear Eric,

It's been a month since I wrote to you. It's been a minute since I thought of you. Today looks much like the day we buried you.

I need your help. I'm worried about Laura. She is so depressed and still feeling guilty about not being able to help you. I would like her to come home to give herself time to heal without the stress of job, school, money, and relationships. Please somehow encourage her to come home. Maybe I'm being selfish but I really need her here with me. And maybe you could come to me and tell me you're okay.

I found a Christmas card I forgot to give you last year. It says, "For a special son, wishing you a Christmas Season filled with friends, family and many warm and wonderful memories. Have a special Christmas. I love you, Mom." I don't know why I didn't give it to you. I don't know why I didn't do a lot of things. Why didn't I help you learn to love yourself? Why didn't I know or understand how much pain you were in? Why didn't you ask someone for help? Why did you drive out into the desert and shoot yourself? Why?

I bought a real Christmas tree for your grave. I'll decorate it with popcorn strings and bird seed and bring it to you on Christmas Eve. You loved Christmas when you were little. You and Laura always tried to find where we hid presents.

Now I want to skip it, make it disappear, go to sleep and not wake up until the end of January. How will I get through Christmas? Through January 7th? Through January 10th? Through another year? I can't write any more. I love you. Mom.

Chapter Three

In Our Dreams

Year One

First things first, I cannot believe it's been a year
Since I've seen your face or heard you laugh.
In twenty years will it feel like twenty years or yesterday?
What is time? You taught me it is now.
Keep visiting me in my dreams so
I can make it through another day.

January 7, 1994

Dear Eric,

I cannot believe it's been a year since you died, since I last talked to you. I should say the last time you talked to me because I talk to you every day. I remember your voice and how upbeat and excited you sounded. You would have made a great actor; you fooled everyone. I'm in Columbus now with my friend Janet, who had a baby girl, Leah Bea, this week. Janet asked me to come and help her for a few days. She also asked us to be Leah's godparents. We were honored and said yes. I feel needed and that I'm not alone on the first anniversary of your death.

Janet's a nervous new mom. I watch her struggle trying to nurse Leah. I remember how easy you were to nurse. I nursed you until you were nine months old and you bit me. I said, "That's it kid, you're getting a cup." I have always wondered if my nursing you caused your stomach problems. One of these days I'm going to write down all the pain you caused me. No, I'm not. That's a part of life; pain, joy, sorrow, sadness, excitement, love, hate, despair, grief, happiness, I could go on.

I wish you had learned that if you wait through one dark feeling, a moment of joy or at least a more bearable feeling will come to you. I hope you are at peace now.

> My son,
> Are you at peace?
> You are at peace.
> One transposed word,
> One hopeful thought.

I miss you so much. In twenty years will I be still missing you? But what is time? You taught me that it is now, this moment, this day. Thank you for that gift. This year is gone but you are not. You are with me always. I gave you life and now you have given me a different life than I planned. Good or bad, our lives are always blesses--if only you had learned that. But you fulfilled your mission. Your death gave me a new understanding, a vision and a mission that I must fulfill. I will continue to write to you. I love you, Mom.

Another workshop I attended at the Common Boundary conference was with Mind/Body doctor Joan Borysenko, Ph.D. She stated, "It is always our wounds that give us our wisdom, the greater the wound the deeper the wisdom. We contract with the angels before we are born what we're here to learn. Of course we're dipped in the water of forgetfulness so we don't remember. We all have a life purpose and it doesn't deal with our 'doing' but with our 'being.' It's about our giving and receiving love. And everyone we meet and every experience we have is a part of our learning about giving and receiving love."

Is that why I'm here with Janet and Leah, to give my love and to just 'be' with them? And do they give their love to me so I can heal and grow and learn and become wise?

I made it through today. If I can do that, I can do any-thing. I am a strong person.

Why couldn't I give Eric that strength? It's too late for him, but not too late to give Laura strength and guidance. She is having a difficult time and needs help. Eric, you can guide her and give her strength to get through this. I know you can. It could be your gift to her. She feels so guilty because you were there with her and she had no idea of the pain you were in. Help her understand why you did what you did. Help her see how special and wonderful she is and the gifts she has to use. Please Eric, help her to learn to live again. And help me.

I read somewhere that in order to move forward we must look back. On this first anniversary of Eric's death I read my "Letters to Eric" journal. In it I found this letter Janet wrote me a couple of weeks after Eric's death. I forgot I asked her to be my memory.

January 22, 1993

Dear Iris,

It's been almost three weeks since we were together and I'm finally taking the time to do as you requested. I am writing down the events of Eric's wake and compiling my thoughts while all the sights, sounds, and smells are still fresh in my memory. I hope this helps you and Jim to move forward and does not cause you too much sadness.

When I arrived on Saturday, you were surrounded by what I think is your core group of wonderful female friends. The conversation was dealing with the recurring question, "Why did Eric take his life?"

We waited for Laura and her dad to arrive as well as your sister, her husband, and son. Through the entire time an astounding theme was laughter. Every five or ten minutes a story about Eric would be told followed by laughter as Eric was always doing something funny. I had a difficult time believing he was so troubled. A comment was made that Eric missed one heck of a party. You and your nephew took a walk and I could see the tears in your eyes when you returned. But you and Jim were strong. Even your dog, Kitty was on her best behavior and knew something was different.

The fireplace burned in eulogy through the days, soothing us all and creating a warm, cozy atmosphere in your living room, comforting us as we gathered to mourn. Eric's pictured was passed around often. Your friends talked of the deep fears this suicide had brought to the surface in us all. Jim had discussions with Carey and Kim, Eric's friends from Phoenix attempting to find an answer. He showed incredible compassion despite his own grief.

The weeks, days, and hours before his suicide were relived over and over in hopes of finding some answers. Because Eric was sexually active, he told a friend he was afraid he might have AIDS. If this was true it could be a believable answer. You would find out when you received the autopsy report. Carey had noticed some depression and was worried about him. No real answers were found and there may never be an answer.

Laura was amazingly strong through all this. She said this will change her and I saw a mature woman walk in that night. Her composure, insights, and deep concerns for her family made her a source of strength for her friends and Eric's friends. I watched her in the church hold you, cry with you and yes even smile with you. She looked so beautiful almost as if to say, "Yes, I want to live."

The calling hours on Sunday were very moving. Eric's picture sat on the closed casket to the relief of many. Flowers filled the over-packed room. You and Jim spoke to over one hundred, two hundred people? Laura and Eric's friends were in shock and kept to themselves or surrounded Laura. The adults tried to comfort them. I remember Jim excusing himself from a conversation to comfort a girl who was having a hard time. The woman he'd been talking to said, "Jim really loves kids."

I spent most of the two hours in the back room watching the nonstop flow of people come and go. Diane and Dan found their way back there, too. This was so much like Diane's son's funeral exactly ten years before. She feared she would sink backwards emotionally in trying to help you. The day after the funeral Diane said she was amazed at how well you were doing. You seemed to draw strength from everyone around you and then turn around and give another person support.

Monday was a day truly created by God. He knew we had been through the most emotion-filled days of our lives. A fog filled the sky allowing us to see only enough and cushion us from the harsh reality at the cemetery. The snow-covered landscape reflected a soft light to give us strength for the task of burying Eric.

The minister's eulogy spoke of the great loss for us and Eric. He did not immortalize Eric but assured us that no matter how wrong it was for Eric to take his own life, God would receive him. It is all right to grieve for our loss because time and faith in God would heal us.

With these thoughts, the procession to the cemetery filed out. The fog surrounded family and friends as they circled the casket and the rectangle hole in the white ground. And the fog surrounded the arms of the unknown. We will hold these four days deep in our memories to remind us that we will survive his loss.

I hope this helps, dear friend. I have fulfilled your request for a written memory of Eric's wake and now would like you to live a full life again. Take a small step forward every minute, every hour, and every day for nowhere does it say you are to stop. We are all here to help. I love and respect you, Jim, and your family.

Sincerely with love, Janet

Journal Entry
May 12, 1994

God and dear Eric answered my prayers. Laura came home for a month. We talked, laughed, and cried about Eric. She visited friends who tried to talk her into staying in Ohio. I pleaded with her to stay but she reminded me she had created a life in Phoenix. A relationship pulled her back. And too, I believe she felt she needed to be with her dad who did not have anyone to help him through his grief. They could do their grief work together.

Dear God and Eric guide her, give her strength and love. I will do the same from here. I say prayers and visualize her getting stronger, recognizing her loving self, and finding her way in the world. I think the guilt of not being there for Eric is still hurting her. I want to write her to encourage her and tell her how much I love her. But I must heal myself in order to help her.

I got a new haircut and don't recognize the woman looking back from the mirror. I cried. Jim made me a nametag so I would know who I am which, made me laugh. I don't feel like that woman looking back from the mirror. I feel frustrated, lost, confused, stupid, lazy, and oh so tired. I feel like I have so much to do but nothing to do. Does that make sense? What is going on? And my mind is racing with a million ideas, thoughts, and feelings. I'm so tired.

Then a simple phone call threw me into the depths of depression. An acquaintance from a woman's organization called and berated me for ten minutes about some insignificant issue I can't even recall. I held the phone to my ear and listened, waiting for her to finish her tirade. After hanging up, I felt uneasy about what took place. The old me would have argued and defended my position, not letting her continue to insult me the way she did. What was wrong with me? I can't do anything right, will I ever be myself again?

I thought when I got through the first-year anniversaries of Eric's birthday, Christmas, and the anniversary of his death, I would feel better. I don't. I feel more depressed and lonely, so worthless.

Is this how Eric felt? Is this why he wanted to die? I'm so tired of crying and complaining. I know my friends are tired of listening to me. I'm tired of listening to me.

Right now I just want to end this pain and be with Eric. Was he this lonely, depressed, and in such pain? I couldn't help him, my son. I can't help my daughter. I can't help myself, so how can I think of helping anyone else? How easy it would be to fill the bathtub and lower my head under the water. I looked at my wrist and wondered if I had a sharp razor. No, I could not put Jim or Laura through more of this nightmare we are now experiencing. Was this the kind of pain, depression, failure, and uselessness that Eric felt?

I cannot put into words the pain I feel thinking of him alone in the desert with these thoughts. I am his mother; I should have known he was hurting.

And then I had that dream, the one where Eric came to tell me to live so I could tell our story. Thank you, Eric.

It was a dream, wasn't it?
You came into the room to tell me a story.
Now I listen, now I understand.
Now I must tell our story.

The next day Northeast Ohio experienced the first solar eclipse seen in 100 years and the next one would not be seen for another 100 years. Everyone was excited and bought special glasses to see it. My friend Carol called to say, "While the eclipse is happening, *write* on yellow paper what you want your life to look like in the future."

Then my friend Diane called to give me a formula for a poem she learned. I put on soothing music and watched the room grow eerily dark as the moon passed across the sun. As others moved outside to witness this majestic event, I went inside to witness my soul.

> There is no death but life.
> I surrender mine to God.
> She will lead me to...light.
>
> A budding flower blossoms.
> A caterpillar metamorphoses and flies.
> She will lead me to...life.
>
> The blossom and butterfly
> Are my soul, my spirit, my life
> They will lead me to...peace
>
> There is no death but life.
> I surrender mine to God.
> She will lead me to...joy.

June 11, 1994

Dear Eric,

I had to visit your grave today. I feel so peaceful here with you. I planted purple petunias. I know you don't like the color but it's my favorite. They'll remind you of me. Your grave looks lovely this time of year with the flowers, the iris star catcher, the little house that says welcome, and the windmill that looks like a cockatoo. Someone left a Mail Pouch tobacco can and a Pittsburg Steelers hat, probably Gabe.

Laura needs your help and guidance. She is having a baby. She's going to keep him/her and raise it alone. She is going to need all the strength and courage that we both can give her. She still experiences heavy grief and guilt from your death. I pray that she will get through all this. She's going to have a tough time but I think this was meant to be. Now that she has another person to think about, she'll start taking care of herself. I wonder if she'll have a boy.

As I planted the petunias I realized I still have anger in me. I'm angry that you're not here with Laura and me. I have to work on that. I remember writing you a letter last year about how angry I was. I even printed it on the computer instead of writing it by hand because I wouldn't be able to read it.

I was angry because you chose to leave me, to die instead of talking to someone, anyone, who could have helped you. I was angry at you for changing my life and giving me so much pain, more pain than your birth ever did.

I was angry at your dad for not seeing your pain the day before you died. I was angry at Laura for being so far away and not wanting to come home and be with me. I was angry at Jim for being so tired and working such long hours that he couldn't comfort me. I was angry at myself for not seeing your pain and not being able to help you. I am still working through this anger but every time a relationship disappoints me, I get angry again and I cry. I miss you and love you, Mom.

> I cried when you were born, my son.
> I cried when you died, my gift.
> I cry today, my inspiration.
> I'll cry tomorrow, my life,
> Tears of joy, instead of sorrow.

I want to write about choices and decisions. Why is it so difficult for me to make decisions even the little ones? What to write about, where to go for dinner, how short should I cut my hair? Bigger ones, where to go on vacation, what color to paint the living room, what kind of car to buy? Then the big one, what should I do for the rest of my life?

Or do I want to do anything? Why is that a question I keep asking? And why can't I answer it? And the one that still haunts me, why did Eric take his own life? How could he, how did he? Did he realize what kind of an effect his last and permanent decision would have on his family, his friends and people he didn't know? I don't believe he did know this or even think about it. If he had, I don't think he would have made that decision. Or would he? That's a question I cannot answer.

About my decisions, how and when did I decide that I needed to write? I've thought about it for a long time but never took action. I wrote my speeches for Toastmaster's and papers for college classes. I remember when I was pregnant with Laura, I thought of writing my thoughts and feelings to this unborn child but didn't. I started many journals but never continued. Not until now when I saw I had to write or I would die. As my New Year's resolution, I began writing letters to Eric. But instead of sending them to him, I write them in a journal. I think I will write him letters until I die.

Maybe what's important is not the decisions themselves but taking action on those decisions. Which is what Eric did. He made his decision and acted on it. He wrote in his suicide note that he was a loser but he finally succeeded in something. I wonder how he feels about that. And now I wonder how Laura feels about becoming a mother? And how do I feel about becoming a grandmother?

Last night my friend, Helen invited me to hear one of her favorite people speak, Naomi Judd. The only things I knew about her were that she sang with her daughter but stopped when she contacted Hepatitis-C and she was beautiful. Helen bought me a copy of her book, *Love Can*

Build a Bridge. We stood in line for her to autograph it, and after hearing her story I wanted to share mine with her. I said, "Last year my 20-year-old son took his own life and now my unmarried daughter is having a baby."

She took my hand and looked me in the eye as she said, "I have a strong intuition that you have a story to tell." She repeated, "You have a story to tell when you are stronger. When the time is right, please tell your story."

Will I know when the time is right? Now I feel like I'm standing still; not moving ahead or going backward, just standing still. I don't like it. I want to keep going. But where, which way, how?

November 21, 1994

Dear Eric,

Happy 22nd Birthday! If you were here I'd buy you a beer. Wouldn't that be a hoot, having a beer with your mom? But here I sit at your grave writing you a letter you will never read. It's sunny but cool and windy today. Not bad for the end of November. I pulled the petunias and planted daffodil and iris bulbs. I hope they take root and grow. You know I don't really garden, but I want your grave to be filled with yellow and purple in the spring. I feel peaceful here today with you. I wish I could stay longer. I know Laura wants to visit you. We'll bring you a decorated Christmas tree. I miss you and I am healing. Love, Mom

Laura is coming home for Thanksgiving and I am excited. We're giving her a baby shower at Walden Country Club with lots of her friends and mine. We're also having Thanksgiving dinner, which we haven't done in ages. We bought a live evergreen tree and are making it our Thanksgiving tree since Laura will not be home for

Christmas. I'll decorate it with pictures of our grandsons Jimmy and Joey, our godchildren Amber, Aric, and Leah, plus little gifts for each of them, including Laura's baby who we call, "Little Phoenix." In the spring, we'll plant the tree in the back yard. Wow, I just realized I'm into planting for some reason, maybe to look to and prepare for the future instead of dwell in the past. Yes, hope for new life and future blessings.

In September I visited Laura to be with her for her first ultrasound. We watched the monitor as a baby appeared, moving slightly. I was nervous and scared for her. My mother's side of the family carries a gene that causes hydrocephalus babies, especially in boys. The technician asked, "Would you like to know the sex of your baby?"

Laura said, "Yes. I had a dream that I'm having a boy." I held my breath. The technician confirmed, "Yes, it's a boy. See that little blimp between his legs?" My daughter is having a baby boy.

I thought about Eric and cried. I cried because my little girl is having a baby. I cried because I miss my son. I cried because the baby looks healthy, no sign of hydrocephalus. I cried because it is a boy and hydrocephalus could still develop. I cried. Unfortunately Laura interpreted my crying as disappointment that it was not a girl. Laura will soon find out as a mother the sex of a baby is not important, only that he's healthy.

It's still difficult for me to look at Jimmy, Joey, and Aric without thinking about Eric. And now that Laura is having a boy, will I see Eric in this baby's face? And it hurts that this little boy will never know his Uncle Eric. Laura assures me that he will.

After a good night's rest, I awoke with a thought. Maybe God is sending this little boy to protect her. And maybe God is sending me a grandson to give me another chance to love and nurture another boy. This thought comforts me.

Chapter Four

The Change

Year Two

First things first, time stood still this swift two years.
I write, I pray, I cry. I wait for "Little Phoenix" to come.
I ask, where will I be in another year?
As sad as I am today?
My missing you still sears my soul.
All the while I know you are with me.
Helping me make it through another day.

January 7, 1995

Dear Eric,
    It's almost midnight. I've made it through the second anniversary of your death. Will I dread January 7ᵗʰ for the rest of my life? I pray not. Laura called. She thought about you all day, still missing you. She imagined what a wonderful uncle you would have been to "Little Phoenix." She cried most of the day. So did I. I thought about that last night I talked to you.
    It's funny. I had a Toastmasters meeting that night and presented a speech about not having enough time to accomplish our goals, but doing "first things first." I used the book The 7 Habits of Highly Effective People, by Stephen Covey. Was some kind of psychic communication happening when you wrote the first sentence of your suicide note, "First things first"? After that, time stood still for me. I cannot write any more. I love you and miss you. Mom

When I can no longer write, read, or walk I listen to music. "On Eagle's Wings" is playing upstairs and "Grand Canyon" playing downstairs. I like the soothing, healing sounds of nature and piano. I relate to the storytelling songs of Louis Armstrong, Barbara Streisand, Carole King, James Taylor, and Harry Chapin. I like some of the oldies that Jim listens to, the Platters, the Kingston Trio, and Patsy Cline. And I can't forget the classics, Bach, Beethoven, and Mozart. I like Jim Brickman, Irish ballads, and Spanish guitar.

At one Common Boundary conference, I spent an entire day with Paul Winter, who brings nature and animal sounds into his music: dolphins, birds, wolves, falling water, and whales. People brought their instruments and we spent the whole day improvising music. Those of us who did not play an instrument used our voices. It was an experience I will never forget.

I love being introduced to songs and singers I've never heard before. At Eric's funeral, his friend Jennifer handed me a tape of a song and asked if we could play it at the service. I did not know the song or artist and asked Rev. Ben. When he saw the title, "Friends," by Michael W. Smith, he said it would be more than appropriate for this celebration of Eric's life. Today when I hear that song, my mind returns to that day and tears return, too.

Once in Toastmasters I presented a speech called, "The Music of My Life." I shared musicals that influenced my growing-up years. I loved Shirley Temple singing "On the Good Ship Lollipop." I pretended it was me singing with my blond curls bouncing as I danced around the living room. I watched "Singing in the Rain" so many times I could feel the raindrops on my face. In high school I performed in "West Side Story." I played Anita and jumped off a barrel in the dance scene so many times I sprained both ankles. My understudy took my part and what really hurt was that she played the part better than I did. I met my ex-husband when I performed in "How to Succeed in Business without Really Trying." He was in the band. When stationed in Spain we lived in the little town where Cervantes was born. "Man of La Mancha" is one of my favorites. My friend and mentor Elizabeth likens me to Liza Doolittle in "My Fair Lady."

My favorite play is "The Phantom of the Opera" which we've seen seven times. The first time we saw it was the first Christmas after Eric died. We drove to Toronto as I did not want to be home that Christmas. I knew the story line but was not prepared for the first song in the second act. When Christine began singing "Wishing You Were Here Again" to her father in the cemetery, I was overcome. I still cry when I hear that song. I continue to listen to music especially when I write letters to Eric. But now I hear Kitty barking, which is another kind of music.

Journal Entry
February 8, 1995

My child is with child.
I take care of her.
Last night I helped her bathe,
Massaged her swollen feet,
Rubbed her tired back,
Read her a bedtime story,
Blew bubbles to give her laughter.
I wish I could soothe her pain.
Soon she will be the mother,
Doing these things for her child.
What will be my task?

Laura's due date has come and gone. She is so big, so uncomfortable, and so ready to deliver this baby. I am at her apartment pool in Phoenix and just talked to John, one of

Laura's neighbors I befriended since I've been here these last three weeks. I told him about Eric and how he died. He said, "The relationship with your daughter has probably strengthened since you've been here. I can see it when you're together. It will grow stronger as the years pass, especially now that she will be a mother." I agree.

Since I've been here, I've mothered Laura. I've rubbed her hurting back, massaged her swollen feet, and read her the story of Coyote Dick whose private parts want to go exploring but end up hopping into a grove of nettles. We laughed and cried.

We talked about how she gave her brother his middle name, Michael. When I went into labor, my neighbor Linda watched Laura until my mother-in-law could pick her up. Laura asked, "Can we name my baby sister Mike?" Yes, her brother's middle name could be Michael after Linda's husband. Eric Michael sounded like a fine name.

Last night I helped Laura bathe. She was so uncomfortable, her feet and hands so swollen she couldn't bath herself. She was a little embarrassed. I said, "Some day when I'm old you will probably have to give me a bath. So remember this time."

"I will, Mom. And thank you for being my mom."

Little Phoenix, come out, come out today.
We are waiting for you, we want to play.
Your mother is anxious to see your face.
It's time to be born, to receive God's grace.

Three days later, I am looking through a two by four-foot window and see five people moving fast and looking concerned but not frightened. They are dressed in green with masks covering their noses and mouths. The only part of their bodies I can see are their eyes, all directed to the woman on the table, my daughter. Her huge belly protrudes like a watermelon and is exposed for everyone to see. Fear and panic surface in me like boiling water. During the last twelve hours she was in labor, I held her hand, rubbed her back, and prayed:

Dear God,

Please be with Laura and this baby. Give her strength, guidance, and courage to get her through this pain and come out on the other side, the side of joy and love. Please help me be a source of strength and love to help her through this. Amen.

After twelve hours of hard labor, the baby's heart rate dropped and the doctor prepared her for an emergency C-section. As I watch the doctor cut into my daughter's abdomen, my heart races. Anything could go wrong, she could die, the baby, too. How could I go on living? I am afraid. My mind races back two years. What is happening to my mind? Where am I? Why can't I stay in the present moment? Is it because the present moment is as painful as the past? I hear a policeman's voice but do not understand what he is saying. Then I hear "Your son is dead." Something about driving into the desert, smoking a cigarette, and shooting himself. A mistake? I hear a scream and then nothing.

I am looking through the window again. I see a baby being lifted from my daughter's belly. The baby cries. He is placed in a bassinet right in front of my window. I count his perfectly shaped ten toes and fingers. He looks so much like Laura when she was born, red faced, with a full head of dark hair. The nurse takes him away. I enter the room. I hold Laura's hand as they sew her back together. I tell her she has a beautiful baby boy. She smiles and falls asleep.

I stayed another two weeks being grandma. I held him close to my heart as I rocked him to sleep singing lullabies. I played with his toes and fingers and read him stories of pirates and heroes and little boys who didn't want to grow up. I think about his Uncle Eric who didn't give himself a chance to grow up and wonder how long I will live in this heavy grief.

I've been reading *Women Who Run With Wolves,* by Clarissa Pinkola Estes, Ph.D. She writes that dwelling on trauma is important in healing, but eventually all injury has to be given sutures and be allowed to heal over the scar tissue. "But we now know what humans have known instinctively for centuries; that certain hurts and shames can never be done being grieved the loss of a child through death or relinquishment being one of the most enduring. Telling and grieving resurrect us from the dead zone. We can grieve and grieve hard, and come out of it tear-stained, rather than shame-stained. We can come out deepened, fully acknowledged and filled with life," Estes concludes.

How many times will I have to tell my story? How long will I have to grieve before I resurface from this dead zone I've been living in these past two years? For now I will concentrate on new life; mine, my daughter's, and her son, my grandson Alec Jeffery Llewellyn.

Journal Entry
October 15, 1995

I've been on my healing journey for two years now and have used my journal writing to learn who I was, who I became, and who I am now. I've learned that I am a strong woman by just being around strong women: Laura, Helen, Anne, Diane, Shannon, Janet, Nancy, Sandy, Sara, Iris B. and many others. At times I've wished I could be more like them now-- strong, knowing who they are, and knowing what they want in life. At one time, I was like them.

I realized my dream of graduating from college and starting my own sales and marketing business. I wanted to become a better speaker so I joined Toastmasters, an international speaking and leadership organization, and started one in my community. I saw I had been a good mother as both my children were becoming adults and finding their own way in life.

Then my son killed himself. I was still a mother but what kind? Did I have to redefine the kind? It was so shameful. This grief work punched me in the gut, reminding me of my daily pain. I didn't know whether I could go on, and if I did who would I be? I wrote in my journal:

It's time for me to find out who I am, what I'm all about and time to move forward. If I died tomorrow, what would my obituary say? What can I give birth to in my life that will enable me to leave this earth with a sense of completion? Can I live my life today as if I might never see another tomorrow? Can I spend time being aware of God's presence, to experience a time of inactivity which can be a time of preparation for gaining strength, wisdom, and insight?

One night when I couldn't sleep, I found a book on my bookshelf, *The Path of Transformation; How Healing Ourselves Can Heal the World,* by Shakti Gawain, and began reading. In the preface of the book, she asks the reader to answer this question: What is my vision of my future? How do I feel about it?

A yellow, lined sheet of paper fell from the book, dated April, 1991. I had written:

I see my future as an exciting adventure in which I am continually learning, striving to know more about myself, and my world. I know that I have so much to do on myself and my world so I see myself living a long time. Right now I am healthy and fit. I am an important part of my family, my children, friends, and people I haven't met yet. I am prosperous not in money but in life. I work hard but enjoy it so it's not work at all. I help others become successful, am an inspirational and motivated leader. I love meeting new people. I grow more physically fit as I grow older. In fact, as my birthdays come and go, I grow younger in mind, body, and spirit.

Today, October 15, 1995, I write: I am a loving and caring companion to Jim, and our love grows stronger every day and year. My life is full as we travel and I share my story with others and hear their stories. I help others in their grieving and growing process. I want to tell my story in writing and speaking. I want God to guide, strengthen, and motivate me to do the work I contracted to do on this earth. I feel excited and joyful about my glorious future.

What is my vision of the future of my community, country, humanity, the natural environment, the planet? This is a little more difficult because I am always so wrapped up in myself and my life. I do see myself more involved in my community, even a leader in an area. I see myself going to schools to talk to students about life, death, and choice. But I know that I must heal myself before I can heal the world. I have much to do.

I have begun. Last year I attended a Survivor of Suicide Conference in Lexington, Kentucky. A woman whose husband took his life organized the conference to bring people together: experts on suicide; mental health practitioners; and those who have lost loved ones to suicide, Survivors of Suicide. A panel of survivors of different relationships answered questions about their experiences and what helped them in the healing process. I met Sandy Martin, a lively, lovely, energetic, passionate, and compassionate woman whose only child, Tony, ended his life several years before. She is from Atlanta and had a deep Southern accent. We found a connection in both losing young sons, but also in our similar personalities and willingness to help others. She invited me to Atlanta to participate in their Suicide Support Team Training that trains survivors to offer comfort and support to recent survivors of a loved one's suicide. My brother lives in Atlanta. I saw I could combine a visit with him and the training.

Sandy introduced me to Iris Bolton, a pioneer in suicide work since her 20-year-old son took his life in 1977. In those days very little information or help was available. Iris became that help and lifeline to others, a beacon of light and a trail blazer for much of the work on suicide awareness and education in the past 30 years. She authored the book *My Son, My Son* that has helped thousands like me get through this nightmare and learn how to live life again. Today the Atlanta Survivor of Suicide community calls me "the other Iris."

I read, learned, and saw that I had experienced the phases of grief: shock, denial, bargaining, guilt, anger, depression, resignation, and acceptance and hope. We do not experience them in a linear manner or necessarily experience all of them. We can move between them, experiencing two or three in a day, in an hour, or even in minutes. This is why we feel like we're going crazy and can't think straight.

At this training I learned about the Four Tasks of Grief. First, we must tell our story and tell our story until our heart and our head understand that it really happened. We must tell it until we don't have to tell it any longer for ourselves but we can tell it to help others. Second, we need to express our emotions. Intuitively, I started writing letters to Eric in my journal to express my emotions. Third we want to make meaning from our loss, to celebrate our loved one's life. I do this every time I tell Eric's story. Finally, our relationship moves from physical to a symbolic or spiritual relationship. Again my letters to Eric helped me with this transition. I still have a relationship with Eric, just a different one.

After the intensive training, I realized it was time to form a Survivor of Suicide support group in my community. I had attended several but they were so far from my home. When one is in heavy grief, energy and effort to drive an hour to a meeting he or she doesn't want to attend is too much to even think about. There had to be others in my area who needed support and healing. After much planning and help from Amie and Ruth, I started a local Survivor of Suicide support group at Townhall II in Kent, Ohio, which provides a 24-hour crisis hot line in our county. How many more firsts will I begin?

November 21, 1995

Dear Eric,
Your 23rd birthday! I dreamed about you last night. You were the age you were when you died. We were together somewhere in the Caribbean, a place we'd never been together before. We were at an aquarium that was attached to the ocean. We watched the blue, yellow, and rainbow fish swim out into the ocean. We met someone we didn't know but enjoyed talking to him. It was a happy dream and I woke up smiling. I'm so afraid I will forget what you looked like. I'll display more pictures of you.
I still find it difficult to believe you are not here. Will I feel this way every day for the rest of my life? I wonder what you would be doing now. I wonder what my life would be like. What would Laura's life be like? But the reality is that you are dead. All I have is my memories of you and your spirit guiding me. Is that enough?
I had a Survivor of Suicide meeting last night. I thought about the night you died and shared it with the group. The phone calls we made, all the people at the house, the stories we shared and the pain. In telling, I felt again the pain that hurt my heart and throat that night, still fresh after almost three years. Someone said, "It seems like yesterday and it will be my yesterday for the rest of my life."
Please visit me more often in my dreams. Love, Mom.

Year Three

First things first, I did not write today.
I went out into the sunshine.
I watched Kitty sit in a trance and
thought about a dying friend.
I took down the Christmas tree and thought of you.
Something is happening inside, like I'm being reborn.
I feel excited, nervous, and scared but I know
That I will make it through another day.

Year Four

First things first, I woke up at 3:30 am and
heard God talking to me.
He said I have a poem that must be written.
I light the angel candle I found on your grave and try to see
your face as
I hold your picture and read your letters.
I think of you and cry. Come to me in a dream,
I want to tell you to forgive yourself
So I can make it through another day.

Year Five

First things first, the phone rang at 12:30 am and
I thought it was you.
But you've been dead and gone these last five years.
I lay in Jim's arms for a while and cried.
I put purple tulips and a white wishing stone on your grave.
I jumped up and shouted, "The time is now for me to howl!"
I made it through another day.

Year Six

First things first, I kept the page but threw the year away.

I listen to the chimes and look out onto the white world.
The one like the day they lowered your body into the ground.
It was only yesterday but
I feel a shiver as I watch the circle grow.
I hear "Amazing Grace," which strengthens and blesses me
And carries me through another day.

Year Seven

First things first, the sun is shining. I do not cry.
I write a poem that brings forth healing.
I will make it through this day.

Part Two

Surviving

Chapter Five

Unwritten

January 7, 2001

As I watch the plastic snowman spin in the snow,
I wonder about you, where did you go?
Why did you choose to die?
The question still haunts me, I cannot lie.
I look out at the white world and know.
You are the snowman singing, spinning in the snow.

Dear Eric,

This day again, another anniversary of your death. Eight years since I've seen your face, heard you tell me the same joke for the tenth time, watched you change the oil in your car, or heard you say, "I love you, Mom." Eight years without you, still missing you but growing stronger, I think, with each passing year.

Today I begin training to walk a marathon in May. It's a fundraiser for the Leukemia and Lymphoma Society. Each participant is assigned an honoree who is our inspiration. My honoree is Zachary, ten years old and in remission. I met him yesterday. Just thinking about what he's gone through in his ten years will keep me walking 26.2 miles and not give up.

I wish you had not given up. I wish you were still alive and walking with me. I wish you would visit me in a dream again so I can see your face, but you are always with me in my mind and heart. I love you. Mom

Our group of six walks in silence for a few minutes. We are freezing. Thick snowflakes stick to my glasses, preventing me from seeing clearly the person in front of me. I think it's Kathy Walker, our walking coach. Yes, that really is her name. Today is our first training day to prepare for the marathon we're walking in May.

"What made you decide to walk a marathon?" Kathy asked, as she paused to walk beside me.

"Last year I wrote in my journal, 'I want to walk a marathon.' A couple of weeks later, a brochure for the Team-In-Training arrived in the mail. When we send a request out to the universe, it responds though I didn't realize it would respond so quickly."

"Do you know anyone with leukemia or lymphoma?" she asked.

"No, but walking helped me heal emotionally, and now it's time for me to help someone heal. Plus, I wanted a goal to work towards to get in good physical shape."

We had been walking fast and saw that the others were trailing behind.

"I'm going back to check on the others," Kathy said. "I'll see you later."

I continued walking. I wore three layers of clothing and felt like the fat snowman I used to make with the kids. I thought about all the walking I've done in my life. I wonder how walking this marathon might change me and where it will lead me.

I have always walked, always. If I squint my eyes real tight and stretch my brain, I can see myself as a one-year old taking a few first steps before tumbling down. But even then I got right up and walked. I've been walking ever since.

For me, walking is not just an effective and inexpensive exercise; it is an emotional, meditative, healing, and even magical experience. The Zulu language has 120 ways of saying "walking." I discovered the healing attributes of walking November 22, 1963, when President John Kennedy was assassinated. The world stopped as we glued our eyes to the television. Eight hours later, I could no longer watch and took a walk under the starry night. I saw Orion looking down as he had for millions of years and he comforted me. Our world would never be the same, but it would go on.

Two years later, while driving home one night, a truck broad-sided me. A three-week hospital stay with broken ribs, pelvis, leg, and head injuries ended my carefree senior year in high school. I wore a cast on my leg for the next six months until the day before I graduated. In the picture receiving my diploma, you can almost see the cane under my graduation gown. That summer I walked and walked. I walked the five miles to my Aunt Betty's house and back. I walked on the railroad tracks for balance. I walked until my limp disappeared and I could pass the physical to enlist in the U. S. Air Force. Marching replaced walking.

I walked the streets of the Spanish village, Alcala de Henares where my husband and I were stationed to await our daughter's birth. I pushed Laura in the stroller and walked the sidewalks of Painesville, Ohio, waiting for Eric to be born. When they were young, I walked my children to the park to play, and as they grew, I walked in order to have time alone.

After Eric's death, my body begged to move. I walked, this time daily with our dog, Kitty. While walking, I cried, screamed, prayed, talked to God, talked to Eric, cried, talked to Kitty, recited poetry, wrote poetry, and cried. With each step, I felt I was healing, just as I did after graduation in 1966. I wrote my first healing poem.

While Walking

While walking, I find an acorn.
Its perfect shape I see
Spinning like a top
Someday will be a tree.

While walking, I find a rock.
Rough, hard, I hold it in my hand.
In one instant, a thousand years pass,
I am left holding sand.

While walking, I hear a robin sing.
I recognize the joyful song.
I wonder if in its world
Does anything go wrong?

While walking, I see my reflection.
My face looks back from a pond.
Startled and scared. In my hand,
I see that I hold a magic wand.

I tap the acorn and the rock; there's the robin.
I see the tree, feel the sand, and hear the song.
I recognize the woman looking back,
She is beautiful, healthy, and strong.

In *Angels of Mercy,* Rosemary Ellen Guiley describes "Be an Angel Day," which began on August 22, 1993. Angels chose August because it is the eighth month of the year, which in numerology is the number of achievement, accomplishment, and fulfillment. Eight is the master number God, the master architect of us all. August is also the month of my birth and is there any meaning in the fact that Angel Day was born the same year my son died?

Now eight years later, what have I achieved, accomplished, or fulfilled? I don't cry every day. That's an accomplishment. I can say Eric's name without tearing up. I speak to other survivors and I've talked to students about choice and living. I still write letters in my journal to Eric.

Guiley says that angels are with us at all times especially, at our birth and death. I'd like to believe that an angel was with Eric on his last moment in the desert. They're with us in our life struggles, experiences, and healing. Is it true that God sends suffering so we can prosper and grow spiritually? That if we have been given a difficult life, we have a fortuitous chance to learn from these difficulties? Are our troubles there to test our faith? Did Eric grow spiritually from his troubles? How will my faith be tested more? Will I ever be able to answer these questions?

Guiley goes on to say that sometimes spirits get trapped and go into limbo. This is what happens when a person takes his own life. But we can intercede by our prayerful thoughts for them and then their spirits are released to heaven. Did I subconsciously speed this process when I started writing letters to Eric? Did I think that I could somehow reach him in limbo, a place where I cannot and do not want to go yet?

I still have much to do on this earth. Is telling my story and Eric's story one of the reasons I am here? At a Common Boundary conference I attended a workshop with Deena Metzger author of *Writing for Your Life.* She asked us to imagine we are at the end of our life. "Without hesitation, without thinking write the story you have lived in five sentences."

My life's story is one of pain, guilt, suffering, unknowing, but also of joy, belief, learning, growing. It's filled with friends, loves, life, and joy. It's a story of growth, exploration, and learning about life, mine and others. In time and turmoil, I learn to live fully and to laugh and love. I struggle not to rage, but to focus my energy on giving back to the world and on making a difference through compassion, forgiveness, laughter and creativity. My story is every woman's story, yet we must each tell our own individually textured stories.

May 1, 2001

"COME TO THE EDGE."
"We can't. We're afraid!."
"COME TO THE EDGE."
"We can't. We will fall!"
And they came.
And he pushed them.
And they flew.

Guillaume Apollinaire

Dear Eric,
I feel as if I'm in training for something more than this marathon. It's giving me energy, a sense of purpose, and discipline, of accomplishing something great, of making a difference. What it is I do not know yet. But I know you are with me every step I take. Thank you, Eric. Love, Mom

In February I visited Laura, now married with another son, Cameron, and a daughter, Sierra. They still live in Phoenix and I miss them every day. But I visit at least once a year.

This visit I did something I've wanted to do for a long time, hike Squaw Peak, now called Piestewa Peak. I was so excited I forgot to eat breakfast, just coffee and a banana. Before I reached the top, I got so weak that I almost fainted. Stopping every few minutes to catch my breath, I reached the summit. Sitting on a flat rock, I looked down at the city and thanked God for my healthy body. This peak so close to the city attracts many experienced and amateur hikers. I carried my camera and asked a woman to take my picture, telling her I was training for a Leukemia Society marathon.

She had walked the San Diego marathon for her husband, a leukemia survivor.

Walking down proved to be as challenging as going up. After a long hour, I felt flat desert, starved and having to pee. If I can hike Squaw Peak, I can walk 26.2 miles.

I visited my friend Diane the other day. She said, "Iris, you've lost weight, look younger and different!" I do feel different: energetic, optimistic, peaceful. In training for this marathon, I'm doing something to make a difference in my physical and mental well- being. My effort is making a difference in my community and my world. I don't know why yet, but it's important to me to do that and to know that.

I haven't felt this good since Eric died. And I fear I shouldn't feel this good. Something terrible might happen again and turn my world upside down. But I'm stronger, and if I can walk a marathon, I can do anything maybe even write a book. Have I ever written those words before?

I want to write a book that will help others to heal and grow, to find a reason to live a full life. I want to write poetry from the heart, poetry that speaks to others who are hurting. I want to be a catalyst for others in their healing journey. In a small way I believe I have, but I want to do more.

May 4, 2001

A significant yet uneventful day. I don't have to walk or train. I don't have to do anything but gather my strength, will power, love, dedication, devotion, courage, and determination. I am ready to walk the marathon tomorrow. I received responses from the E-mail I sent out: "Good luck, we'll be thinking of you. You can do it!" Even so I'm getting anxious and nervous. Can I really do this? YES, I CAN! Why? To raise money and help find a cure for leukemia. To help Zachary, my hero and inspiration, and others like him to live long, healthy lives. To get into shape. To see if I can do it. To heal a little more.

But first I have to get through this wedding. Beth, Eric's high school sweetheart, is getting married today.

Emotionally I could not get through the ceremony but will attend the reception. I am happy that Beth found someone to love who also loves her. I know Eric loved her in his way. The last sentence in his suicide note was, after all, "Tell Beth I'll always love her." I will get through this evening and tomorrow.

It's supposed to be sunny and in the 70's, perfect for a walk. My friend Chris is coming to do my hair. If nothing else, I'll look gorgeous. I hope I'm ready; I've been training for four months, and now it's time to perform. I CAN DO IT! I WILL DO IT! Tomorrow I will be a different person. I will be a woman who walked a marathon, 26.2 miles!

May 5

Last night, after Beth's reception I fell into bed exhausted and excited. I woke up at 2:00 am, then 3:00, and 4:00 and finally at 4:15am. I got up and into the shower, then filled my fanny pack with granola bars, an apple and an orange, my walkman and tapes, camera, pen and paper, Kleenex, and wipes. Still dark when we left but traces of the sun appeared, promising a clear day but cold so early in the morning. I'm glad I wore my jacket. We found the Team-in-Training tent where Kathy, Fred, Rachel, and Sherrie were shivering but excited. As the sun rose, 1,500 runners and walkers crossed Cleveland's Detroit-Superior Bridge. In a sea of purple shirts, I walked: across that bridge through Ohio City to Tremont, then back across the Hope Memorial Bridge where Jim was waiting on the other side. We kissed quickly as I continued walking: down Euclid Avenue, to 40th Street, then out Chester all the way to the turnaround at Shaker Square where Jim was having lunch with our friends Lin and Fran. I kissed and hugged them and continued on. I stopped at a church to use the bathroom. I walked with our group, with people I hadn't met, and sometimes I walked alone. I walked and walked. In University Circle close to the art museum, I saw Chris, who had joined Jim and our friends. Again, hugs and kisses all around and good-byes until we would meet at the finish line.

I walked alone through Rockefeller Park until PJ, a volunteer, asked if she could walk with me for a while. Times speeds nicely when you walk with someone. But I was getting tired and during that last 6 miles I s-l-o-w-e-d to a turtle's pace.

When I saw Lake Erie and Marginal Road, I stepped up my pace; I could feel the finish line beckoning me. My friends met me at the Cleveland Browns stadium to walk the last mile with me. I saw a bearded man taking my picture, then realized it was my brother, Ed. He and his girlfriend Sue surprised me by being there. Then I saw Zach and his dad, holding a sign that said, "Iris, you did it!" As I crossed the finish line, I heard my name called and a water bottle appeared in my hand. I was crying. Everyone was hugging me and Jim was snapping pictures. I felt whole, happy, and alive.

But drinking my celebratory Long Island Ice Tea, I wondered, "What do I do now?"

Chapter Six

I Hear a Call

June 7, 2001

> I hear God's voice say,
> "It's time for you to walk in
> memory of your son."

Dear Eric,

I'm still flying high from completing the marathon. Thank you for being with me. I feel healthy and whole, looking towards the future instead of back to the past. If I can walk a marathon, what else can I do?

I read in the paper that Steve Newman, who walked around the world, is walking from Cleveland to Cincinnati to bring awareness of disabled people. I could do something like that to bring awareness to suicide. Do you think that sounds crazy, Eric? I love you, Mom.

I had a dream.

I was sitting with a woman who asked me, "What are you doing?"

"I'm writing a book." I said.

"What's it about?

"It's about a healing journey. No, not just healing, but surviving, and thriving and growing stronger with each step I take, with each journal entry and poem I write, and each time I tell Eric's story."

She walked away. Then God sat down next to me and said, "It's time for you to walk in memory of your son and then write a book about it."

I woke up sweating.

What did that mean? Yes, I just walked a marathon, but now where am I supposed to walk? Was God really talking to me? And what am I supposed to say to Jim?

I'll think about it tomorrow. Right now my back hurts! I need to see my chiropractor, Tony. After examining me and suggesting a few treatments and exercises to get my back healed, I ask him, "What kind of exercises should I do to get into shape for a long walk?"

"How long a walk?"

"I'm not sure. Maybe 1,000 miles or more."

"Wow! Where are you going?"

"I'm thinking about walking to Phoenix."

"That's more than 1,000 miles, more like 2,000 miles. But you can do it."

He gave me some exercises for upper-body and back strength and stretching exercises. While I lay on the back rolling machine, I mentioned my idea to a woman on the rolling machine next to me. I was so excited, I had to tell someone.

"I'm thinking about a project I'd like to pursue to bring awareness to an issue that's important to me."

"What is it?" she asked.

"I want to walk in memory of my son who took his own life. It's important to bring awareness to suicide and its impact on loved ones left behind."

Silence.

"That's a subject people don't want to talk about, but you're right- we need to talk about it. Good luck on your journey."

The more I thought about it, the more excited I became. I could walk from Eric's grave in Chardon, Ohio, to the place he died in the desert just outside Phoenix to raise awareness for suicide prevention. Is this totally outrageous and unrealistic? I have to get all the information and details before I approach Jim with the idea. He'll think I'm crazy, I have to find the exact mileage-- it's about 2,000 miles. If I walked fifteen to twenty miles a day it would take me three and a half to four months. People take six months to walk the Appalachian Trail, so my idea isn't that unrealistic.

The more I thought about it the more excited I got. I could contact people I know along the way like Frieda and the Ericson's in Missouri. Who else? I could write about it the way Shirley MacLaine wrote about her pilgrimage in *The Camino, A Journey of the Spirit*. My spiritual journey would be my pilgrimage to heal myself and to help others see the emotional fallout from suicide.

I can do this. Yes! Yes! Yes!

June 19, 2001

We celebrate our thirteenth anniversary at our favorite place in Ohio, Put-in-Bay on South Bass Island in Lake Erie, the Key West of the North. This one-by two mile island is home to 350 year-round citizens and the number soars to 10,000 a day in busy summers. Catawba Street, lined with Victorian homes, shops, hamburger joints and a wine-basted chicken patio entices shoppers and hungry folks of all ages.

Music pours from the Round House, the Boat House, the Crescent Tavern, Tippers, and the Beer Barrel Saloon, which has the longest bar in the world. Across the street kids play in De Rivera Park while boaters party on the decks of boats docked in the harbor.

Since 1987, we've spent a week in the summer on this island resting at the Vineyard Bed & Breakfast, owned by Mark and Barbie who we now call friends. Built in 1865, this Victorian beauty sits on twenty acres of land, six of which are a vineyard overlooking Lake Erie.

This warm, sunny June day we ride our bikes to Heinemann's Winery and sit at a picnic table sipping a Sweet Catawba. Since it's our anniversary, we sit alone instead of striking up a conversation with the people at the next table.

"I have something I need to tell you."

"Okay, honey, what is it?"

"You remember how I felt after the marathon, how healthy and whole the first time since Eric died?"

"Yes, and you look wonderful because of it. The marathon was life changing for you."

"I want to do something else that will change my life."

"What is it?"

"I want to walk from Chardon to Phoenix in memory of Eric."

Silence. Jim gets up from the table and walks away. He's gone so long I wonder if he's going to come back. After about ten minutes, he returns, sits down, and takes my hands in his.

"I'm sorry I had to leave. I didn't know what to say to you. I thought about all the reasons why you shouldn't do this. It's a crazy idea. It will take three to four months, can your fifty-three years-old body do this, how much will it cost? Then I realized this was something you had to do and I had to do it with you. I say yes, let's make this journey together and have fun doing it."

From that minute, we began to plan our pilgrimage.

November 21, 2001

"In a few years you will sing a song."
I said, "No, you are wrong.
How could I sing?" I cried.
My son has died.
"In a while, you will learn to smile.
You will laugh as well as cry,
But you will never say good-bye.
He is not on this earthly plane,
But you will be together again.

65

Until that time, laugh, sing, and live.
And experience all the love you can give."

Dear Eric,

Today is your 29th birthday. It seems strange to not visit you at the cemetery today. Instead, we drove to Chicago to spend Thanksgiving with Scott. I didn't get sad. I even sang a song this morning. I am healing.

It's warm for November and I need to go for a walk. I love walking in Chicago; it's so different from home. People walking, running, riding bikes, shopping in crowds, exotic aromas from ethnic restaurants. I feel like I'm lost in a foreign country. It seems all I've been doing this year is walking, walking, weight training, yoga, and riding my bike. Did I tell you that one of our friends suggested I bike so I could go more miles in a day? At first I resisted.

Then I remembered you loved to bike. I decided to bike for you and walk for me. I'm feeling physically stronger, making me mentally stronger. Will I be strong enough to walk and bike across the country to the Southwest next year?

Time for that walk. I think I'll walk up to Lincoln Park and along Lake Michigan. I love the Chicago skyline. I love you and miss you, Mom.

We've had a busy summer. I started two-year training in Washington, D.C., to become a CPT, Certified Poetry Therapist. In my grief work, I discovered the healing powers of reading and writing poetry. I found the form, language, rhythm, images, and metaphors of poetry a meaningful way to express my emotions. I was practicing poetry therapy before I realized such a profession existed.

Then I read an article in our local paper announcing a workshop in April 2001 by Poetry Therapist John Fox. I had to attend. I learned about the National Association of Poetry Therapists (NAPT), which provides educational programs, conferences, and certification requirements for Certified and Registered Poetry Therapists who work in schools, hospitals, nursing homes, and hospices. I researched the requirements and realized I wanted to help others heal through reading and writing poetry. I wrote this poem in John Fox's workshop.

And I Knew

I remember that day swinging high into the sky,
Wishing I could take hold of that black crow who
Would fly me back to you.

And I knew...

I remember that day trying to stay awake while
Mr. Blake talked about some war where men died,
And the loudspeaker said our president is dead.

And I knew...

I remember that day I thought what fun
A new year had begun a chance to start again.
A policeman came to the door and said, "Your son is dead."

And I knew...

In July I flew to Washington, D.C., to begin my poetry therapy training. On the plane I met a young woman from Middlebury College. I told her about my pilgrimage. In fancy printing she wrote in my journal:

Adventure-- Your life is a grand adventure. Take risks. Explore the unknown. Journey forth into the great, wide open without prepared outcomes. Go for it.

Below the message she drew a picture of an angel.

My horoscope that day in *The Washington Post* was: Be amenable to change, travel and have a wide variety of experiences.

Is the universe encouraging me, making my pilgrimage real?

In one session at the training, we did a meditation before writing. Eric visited me, reminding me of an idea I wrote in my journal just after he died: to speak, write, and share my story with others to help them not make the decision he made. The idea came to me that I could share my poetry and journal writing with others to help them heal. I could tell our story as I walk and bike across the country.

After the training, Jim and I drove to Southern Pines, North Carolina for two months to spend time with Jim's dad. I spent my 53 birthday there and wrote about what I want this year to look like:

Healthy body.
Working mind.
Questions answered.
Jewels to find.

And then it was September 11, 2001. The world stood still, watching in horror as two planes hit New York's World Trade Center, another hit the Pentagon, and a third crashed in a field in Pennsylvania. I could not watch television. I cried and walked and prayed. I felt the shock, pain, grief, sorrow, guilt, and anger of the thousands of survivors who will descend into the well of grief today. My grief resurfacing, I pray for the thousands of survivors who will be traveling this path. New grief revives my old grief, but I cannot go to January, 1993 right now.

I remember that warm day the sun shone from God's heaven,
Then looped pictures imbedded our minds, two planes crashing into two towers,
Buildings burning, bodies falling, our world tumbling.

And I knew...

Chapter Seven

There You'll Be

January 7, 2002

Dear Eric,
The ninth anniversary of your death looks like the day
we buried you. New snow covers the ground; tiny flakes
whiten a bleak day that looks like the end of the world. But
then I remember that spring comes again and life goes on as
it has these past nine years. I thought of you when I went to
sleep last night and I thought of you when I woke this
morning.
What do you think about my walking and biking to
Phoenix? Pretty crazy, huh? But I know I'm supposed to do
it. I'm excited and need to work hard to get in shape. I'll be
54 when I begin. Will my body be strong enough? I know
you'll be with me every step of every mile. I feel you are
encouraging me and I now know you are okay. I'm reading
Conversations with God Book 3, in which Neale Donald
Walsch asks God if our loved ones who died are okay. And
God replies that they are very okay.
I know you are okay, probably more okay than you've
ever been. And I'm more okay than I've ever been because
I'm finally doing my life's best work, the work you left me to
do. And using the gifts you helped me realize I have:
speaking to others about life and choice; writing and
teaching poetry; sharing our story to help others heal; and
listening to others' stories. I found this in a letter I wrote to
you in July of 1993:
What gifts have you given me, Eric? You taught me to
be more understanding and compassionate. I've read that to

help heal others you must first heal yourself. That's why I'm working on getting stronger-- you gave me the gift to help others, especially those who have lost a loved one to suicide. You knew I was strong and would survive your suicide. But I must do more than simply survive day to day; I must heal and become stronger to be ready for whatever it is I am here to do. You gave me the realization that I have been in training all my life for a purpose that will help others and make a difference in this world. I'm not sure how yet.

I miss you and wish you were here to make me laugh. Making people laugh was your special talent. You really did give us love and laughter. I wish you were sitting right here with me here now. I wish I could change things. I wish, I wish, I wish.

Thank you, Eric, for reminding me of your gifts and talents. And now it's time to get to work and start using my talents. I love you and miss you, Mom.

April 29, 2002

Dear Eric,

I have been so busy I haven't written you in a while. Every day I walk, bike, and do exercises to strengthen my body for this adventure. In addition to that I'm studying for my Certified Poetry Therapy certification, and taking a Healing and Poetry class at Lorain Community College, and also tutoring a couple of students, including a woman from Japan. Oh, and I'm working with a grief group. No wonder I haven't written.

But I'm excited about my life. I feel I am making a difference. I have no idea how this pilgrimage will change me but I know it will. Oh, we're in Denver, Colorado. Love, Mom

She says, "Honey, I want to go to Denver,
Would love to have you come.

Share my dreams. Share my passion."
He says, "Love to, I'll be there to
Share our dreams and live our passion."

"We need to talk," Jim says nervously.
"Yes, we do," I agree.
We're sitting at the Hard Rock Cafe in downtown Denver enjoying our time together. Every year after tax season we take a trip. Sometimes we fly to a distant place like Cancun. Sometimes we go to Toronto, commit to a wedding in Nebraska, or enjoy time at a Bed & Breakfast close to home. This year I enticed Jim to come to Denver with me to attend the National Association for Poetry Therapy conference as I need the hours for my CPT certification. While I'm attending workshops, Jim relaxes and begins working on the website for our journey. We hope our friends will follow us on the internet while we walk and cycle across the country.

Jim's been out of sorts for a couple of days. He always goes through a transition right after tax season. Going from 60-70-hour work weeks for four months down to the normal 40-hour work week takes him a few weeks to adjust to. I know he's been thinking about the journey we plan to start on August 18 just around the corner. This would give us three months to reach Phoenix by Eric's 30 birthday on November 21. I'm nervous, too. What if my body can't do it?

"I've been thinking about this pilgrimage, as you're calling it. Iris, I'm worried we're not going to be ready. Also I'm not sure I can be away from the office for the three months that it's going to take you. I know how important it is and I want us to do it, but let's talk about dividing it into parts. What do you think?"

"What I think is relief. I've been worried about it too. I'll turn 54 just before we leave. Yes, I've been walking ten miles a day, riding my bike, lifting weights, going to yoga and Pilates classes. But am I ready? And can I finish 2,000 miles without injuring myself?"

"What if we divide it into three parts and do one part every summer?" he asks.

"That would take three years. Could we keep the passion and excitement for three years?"

"Let's look at the map and consider the times of the year and weather conditions."

"Sounds good to me."

Our compromise was one we both could live with. We would begin this August 31, Labor Day weekend. We'd take about a month to go from Chardon, through Ohio, Indiana, and Illinois, ending in St. Louis, Missouri.

The next phase would begin in June, 2003, starting in St. Louis and going through Missouri and Oklahoma, ending in Amarillo, Texas. The middle of October we'd complete the journey from Amarillo through the rest of the Texas Panhandle, New Mexico, and Arizona, arriving in Phoenix on Eric's 31st birthday. We both felt good about this plan.

June 11, 2002

Dear Eric,

I'm here having lunch with you at your grave. One last light purple iris and red geranium still bloom. The wind blows the chime and the breeze feels refreshing in the hot sun. A man is mowing the grass nearby but shuts off the mower and walks toward me as I lay my blanket down.

"I've seen you here before and always want to say hello. My name is High."

"Hi, High. I'm Iris. How long have you worked here? "

"Over thirty years. I'm retired now but still work part time. That your boy?" He points to your grave.

"Yes"

72

"I buried your boy. It's the young ones I can't handle. I stand and watch the funeral and then walk away until everyone is gone. What happened to him?"

As I tell him the story, I see tears in his eyes.

I get tears when I think how much I still miss you. So much has happened since you died. Laura and I have grown so much. We are closer now because of you. You gave us much in your life but you've given much in your death, too. I cannot imagine what our lives would be like if you hadn't chosen to die.

Despite the pain, no, because of the depth of the pain I believe I am a better person. I have finally learned to love myself. I owe that to you. How can I say thank you for the life you've given me? Thank you, Eric. I wrote a list poem for you. I love you, Mom

What I've learned from Eric's death:

I've learned to give compassion and understanding.

I've learned to live each day to the fullest.

I've learned death transforms a relationship but doesn't end it.

I've learned to say, "I love you" to my loved ones every day.

I've learned I am here for a purpose and must work to achieve that purpose.

I've learned I heal by helping others heal.

I've learned I have talents I haven't discovered yet.

I've learned I need to use those talents to make a difference in my world.

I've learned grief never ends but the pain lessens, not just with time but by what we do with and in that time.

I've learned I still have much to learn.

I've learned I can still help those who have died with prayers and loving thoughts, remembering them every day.

I've learned the greater the sorrow we experience, the greater the joy we can discover.

I've learned life is too short not to enjoy every moment.
I've learned writing down my thoughts produces action I take on them.
I've learned every day is filled with beauty, love, and joy.
I've learned to thank God for all my blessings.

In two months I will learn about walking and biking across the country and telling our story. I wrote a letter to my journey:

Dear Pilgrimage,

I wanted to write to you about you and share you with others, but I haven't. Oh, I talk about you to people. I love their reactions when I say, "In August I'm starting my walk and bike ride from Chardon, Ohio, to Phoenix, Arizona." The looks on their faces reveal wonder, surprise, and just plain, "Is she crazy?" Then I tell them why and their expression changes from admiration and awe to sympathy and sadness. Some say they want to walk with me some of the way, some give me routing suggestions, or they don't believe I'm really going to do it. Most say, "Good luck."

Every day I exercise: walk, bike, do yoga and Pilates. I eat healthy in getting ready for you. In the back of my mind though, a question sneaks in, "Can I really do this, or should I forget the whole thing?"

Then I think about why I'm doing it -- in memory of my son who chose to die. To share my story and Eric's story in hope of helping others whose loved ones made that same decision and left them to suffer and grieve. I also want to have conversations with those who are thinking about ending their lives. I want to tell them that life is worth living, that what is going on in their lives right now might suck but things change-- especially when we find our gifts and purpose. Sometimes it takes a long time to find our gift, the reason we are here.

But if we give up, that chance is gone forever, erased from experience. Deleted.

So I will walk. With each step I will heal a little more and know that someone I meet may need to hear our story. I will walk, I will speak, and I will heal and thereby hope to help someone.

I begin you, my pilgrimage and continue to the end, not just this walk but to the end of my life. Thank you, dear journey.

Journal Entry
August 30, 2002

Jim just left to run some errands. He's taking today off to pack the car and get ready for tomorrow. I need to write for a few minutes.

Tomorrow at this time I will have walked for a couple of hours. I can't believe the day I begin this pilgrimage is almost here. I hope it's sunny and warm like today. I'm nervous. My hands are shaking, but I know I am supposed to walk. I have lots of supportive friends who are praying for our safe journey. I received a card from Laura that made me cry and a birthday card from Jim's dad with $10 in it. I need to find some pictures of all our grandchildren and godchildren to take with me. So many last-minute details. I should make a list.

Helen sent me a CD of songs called "Songs Inspired by Literature." One song grabbed me, "Tell Your Story Walking," by Deb Talan which was inspired by the book *Motherless Brooklyn, by Jonathan Lethem.* The chorus goes:

> Tell your story. (Tell it, tell it.)
> Tell your story to anyone who will listen.
> Tell your story, don't stop talking.
> Just tell your story walking.

I also read both of Lou Suarez's poetry books. I loved them. I met him last week at the writing conference I attended. I arrived late because I got lost. I always do when I go to the west side of Cleveland. But many others did too, so it started late. I sat in the front next to one of the speakers, Lou Suarez. I found out he was judge for the poetry contest that I had forgotten I entered last summer.

I opened my conference packet and there was my poem all marked up with red comments that I could not read. I asked if he could interpret them some time during the day. I went to his session where he shared what makes a good poem and read some of his poems. After lunch I saw him sitting alone and asked if he could go over my poem. He gave me some great suggestions and I plan on revising it.

Then came the awards. They offered first, second, and third place awards for fiction, non-fiction, science fiction, children's, and poetry. When Lou called my name, "Iris Llewellyn Angle for first prize in poetry for 'Night Sky' I was shocked. He shook my hand and presented my certificate and envelope, saying, "I didn't want to give it away when we talked earlier." I was shaking when I read the certificate and opened the envelope with a $50 bill inside. Wow, my first poetry contest-- and I won!

Night Sky
For Alec

Remember the night we
went out to look at the
sky. It was so dark you
did not want to walk too
far into the desert. I found
Orion for you. A fierce
and famous hunter who
the gods defeated because
he boasted too much. They

sent him to the heavens to
guard the night sky. His belt
of three bold stars holds
his strong sword. I did
not tell you that he is
my hero. He was there
the dark night when
I walked away from the
voices that said our
president was dead. He
was there the quiet night
I walked down the road
and wanted to die. He
was in the same desert sky
that black night your uncle
chose to die. He was there
that bright night you were
born, his belt sparkling so.
Orion is here as I hold
your soft hand and we look
up at the night sky.

Tomorrow will be another first as I begin to tell my story walking.

Part Three
Thriving

Chapter Eight

Tell Your Story Walking

August 31, 2002: The First Phase Begins

> Long journey begins,
> Holding hands we say a prayer
> And take the first step.

A surreal sun and cloudless sky greet Jim, Biscuit, and me at the Chardon Cemetery a few minutes after 8:00 am. Several friends are already gathered at my son's grave. The black granite stone that has covered his body for almost ten years shines in the morning sun. The red petunias I planted earlier this summer still bloom. A purple plastic butterfly feigns gathering nectar from one blossom.

Couples from our old church – Jim and Betsy, Sue and Roger -- want to share the beginning of this pilgrimage and give us hugs all around. I see a young man I do not recognize, and then realize it is Gabe, Eric's best friend. With his bleached-blonde hair, he no longer resembles Tom Cruise. His five-year-old son, Jordan, stands next to him. Both gaze at the gray headstone next to Eric's, Gabe's father's grave. Jordan plays hide and seek behind it as Gabe tells him a story about his grandfather. Beth, Eric's high-school sweetheart has brought her friend Tabitha. They look like sisters, both petite. Beth's sandy hair is short and curly while Tabitha's is longer and straight. They appear not to have changed in ten years.

This family of friends forms a circle around Eric's grave. Jim and Betsy say a prayer of thanksgiving, they pray for our safe journey. We stand in silence, each thinking our own thoughts. Mine are on the physical journey I'm beginning today. I'll think about the emotional journey later. For now I just want to think about this walk. Am I physically prepared for this? Is it too late to change my mind? What am I doing?

I shoo away my fears and doubts as I listen to my friend Jim pray for a safe and healing adventure. After long hugs and tears, we say good-bye to Jim and Betsy who head to the Geauga County Fair to sell Jim's pottery. Gabe is taking Jordan to Niagara Falls for Labor Day weekend. The rest of us, including Biscuit, begin walking.

Jim drives the van and will meet us later.

We head south on Rt. 44, an old tree-lined street I walked a hundred times when I lived here. We say good-bye to Sue and Roger and two minutes later, John, another friend, joins us. We turn down Bass Lake Road where I lived for fourteen years, where Eric and Laura grew up. Here I hug Beth and Tabitha good-bye.

I walk past my old house, a long white ranch with two lonely-looking front doors still painted blood red. Does anyone go in and out these doors? The pine trees lining the property are now taller than the house. My ex-husband and I planted them as seedlings and wondered if they would ever grow. Three of the pines were our first three Christmas trees.

My prize planting was the giant weeping willow close to the road. Heavy rains formed a low spot which created a small pond. A friend told me that weeping willows love water. I found what looked like a miniature weeping willow branch and planted it in the dried up pond. Now almost 30 years later as I pass this giant tree, the willow leaves sing softly, "We remember you!"

In memory, I see a blonde boy in glasses sitting on the steps petting a kitten. Eric had begged for a kitten, and then one day someone left a litter on the steps of the office where I worked. Eric chose the name Smokey for his charcoal color. How many Lego houses did Eric build for this kitten before it grew into a cat and disappeared into the woods?

Good-bye, memory of Eric, the white ranch with the two red doors, the weeping willow, and the tall pines.

Our first destination is The Liberty, an assisted-living home where my friend Sara lives. She is in the beginning stages of Alzheimer's and is not sure of what is happening. She says, "Iris, you're crazy for making this trip! But I love you anyway." I hug her and John good-bye. Jim is driving John home and will meet me at the end of the day.

Biscuit and I are alone for the first time. I didn't want another dog. I'm not really an animal person. When Eric was three months old, my ex-brother-in-law showed up at our door with an eight-week-old Shepherd mix puppy. We had just moved into our new house. Laura was three years old, and my mother and sister were visiting for a week. Now was not a good time for a puppy. Yet something told me she would be good for our family.

Heidi became my third child. Wherever the kids went, Heidi went. I fed the kids, I fed her. The kids had to go out, she went out. Eric managed to keep Heidi fed, first with scraps that landed on the floor. As he got older, he fed her the vegetables he didn't want to eat. Just after Eric learned to walk, he discovered the giant front yard and headed for the road. Heidi ran after him and dragged him back into the yard. That day I became a dog person. She lived to be fourteen, old for a Shepherd.

After Heidi died, Laura knew my new husband Jim and I needed a dog. She surprised us with a Christmas present, a Collie mix puppy from the Humane Society.

We had just moved into our new home and didn't plan on getting married until spring. We had enough adjusting to do without adding a puppy to the list.

But how could we say no to this furry little puppy with a red ribbon around her neck? We struggled to find a proper name. We agreed to call her Kitty. Jim thought it would be funny to call, "Here, Kitty, Kitty," and have a dog come running. The people at the Humane Society told Laura that Kitty would grow to about forty pounds--she stopped at sixty.

When Eric died, Kitty didn't eat for four days. She knew someone was missing. She became my walking partner and listened to me cry. Three years ago after cancerous tumors spread throughout her body, we held her in our arms as the vet put her to sleep.

I told Jim I didn't want to talk about another dog for at least two years. We made it to three. As we planned this journey, Jim said, "Iris, how about a dog to keep you company and give you some protection?" Again I felt that was just the right thing for us both.

We made weekly excursions to the local dog shelters, read the papers, and told friends about our search. We did have parameters. We wanted an older dog so we wouldn't have to go through potty training or the chewing-everything-in-the-house stage. We also preferred short hair for little shedding, medium size, good disposition, amenable, traveler, and eager walker. Jim turned to the Internet and found AlterPets, an organization that fosters dogs until they find homes for them. After several searches, we found Biscuit, a medium-sized, Beagle/Shepherd mix, between 2-3years old and cute. She was immediately available for a new home -- ours.

Today Biscuit keeps me company as I begin this 2,000-mile journey. I wonder if she's as scared and nervous as I am. Biscuit and I stop by a pond to collect our thoughts.

> In green water, blue
> heron stands still, speaks to me.
> I stop to listen.

The heron looks straight at me. I feel his eyes bore into mine as if he wants to tell me something I need to hear. I stand, listening and watching him. Time is as though I were pressing the pause button on the video, giving me time to really see the picture. At that moment, I experience just being present to the moment. That's all it was, yet it was everything in one thing.

In Hudson, Ohio, we meet Jim's secretary, Amy, and her three little girls who want to walk with me. Heather is ten and shares Eric's birthday, Caitlin is seven, and Mikayla three. All three seem to be excited to walk with this crazy lady. Bobby, husband and dad, follows in the car in case one of them gets tired before we reach Hudson Square. I am wearing the t-shirt Amy gave me. It's pink with blue lettering giving Eric's full name and the date of his death. Small green, yellow, and blue footprints climb up the back. Wearing it, I feel light and close to Eric.

After saying good-bye to everyone at Hudson Square, Biscuit and I walk down Rt. 303 to McDonald's for a snack and restroom break. Jim meets me there to take Biscuit. It's time to ride my bike to Peninsula, Ohio, a comfortable downhill ride. We begin a routine: Biscuit walking with me a few miles and then she gets in the van with Jim while I bike. He drives five or six miles down the road to wait for me in a restaurant, coffee shop, McDonald's, library or even a garage sale.

I am sweaty and miserable when I reach The Winking Lizard, a favorite restaurant and bar in the center of Peninsula. Jim is inside waiting for me but must not hear his cell phone. I need help putting the bike in the car which he left running with the air conditioner on for Biscuit. Perspiration runs into my eyes and my sweaty hands make it difficult to loosen the axle nut. I get the wheel off and the bike into the car. I walk into the cool, dark bar and order a tall glass of ice water and heave a sigh of relief. After lunch, I walk uphill into Richfield. As the afternoon grows hotter, my breathing and thinking became one as they often do when I walk.

"Walk on. It is important to keep moving. It does not matter how slowly you go, as long as you do not stop."
Confucius

Is that what I've been doing these past nine years, just walking on, moving slowly, and not stopping? But now I'm on a pilgrimage, with a goal to reach. The image of journey, quest, or pilgrimage is a theme in all wisdom traditions. In this quest we explore, question, and come to terms with our shadow self. Naturalist, Loren Eisely calls our shadow self "the ghost continent within." I feel I've been hiding on this inner continent so long the only way to get out and beyond it is to keep walking. As Ohio poet Mary Oliver says in "The Journey," after recognizing our own voice we must go deeper into the world.

Is that what I'm doing now after hiding so many years inside my journal? Yes, I'm going out into the world. As Mother Teresa urges, "Go out into the world today and love the people you meet. Let your presence light new light on the hearts of people." What kind of people will I meet on this journey? Who will need to hear my story? Whose story will I need to hear?

Golden butterfly
Lands on my shoulder, whispers,
"Yes, you can do it."

Our fourth day out is the first day Jim and I will not be returning home for about a month. This day tests our relationship and could have been our last day of the trip. We pack the car and head back to Richfield where we ended yesterday.

Another scorcher on uphill terrain, I walk uphill, bike downhill. When I walk, I wear a baseball cap with Eric's picture and a collection of pins circling it. First, my Team-in-

Training pin I received from the marathon I walked for the Leukemia and Lymphoma Society, along with a pink sunglasses-shaped pin my friend Chris gave me that day. I bought a beaded pin that says, "Live, love, laugh." One last pin my friend Kay gave me reads, "You can do it!" After walking six miles, sweat running down my face, I take off my cap and wipe the sweat from my forehead.

I look at the picture of Eric and his secret grin makes me smile. But the "You can do it" pin is missing! Is this an omen? Does it mean I will not succeed? I start to cry, then stop. It's just a pin. I bless it and let it go, knowing that whoever finds it will need the message more than I do. I continue walking, feeling peaceful, knowing that whatever happens is supposed to happen.

I walk uphill, uphill, uphill realizing how physically active I've always been. When I was little I enjoyed tap dancing, playing with a hula hoop, marching in a band, jumping rope, climbing trees, and riding my bike; anywhere, everywhere, away from where I lived. I discovered there was a world outside of Norwalk, Ohio, and that's where I wanted to be -- gone.

In the Air Force I rode my bike all over Maxwell AFB in Montgomery, Alabama. I walked every street in Alcala de Henares, Spain, the year we spent there. While living in Painesville, Ohio, I rode my bike to Lakeland College. I had a seat on the back for Laura to ride with me. Wow! I have come full circle. Now I'm walking and riding my bike across the country.

The ringing of my cell phone startles me from my reverie. Jim is upset. Five miles down the road, he stopped at a cemetery to put the wheel on my bike, preparing it for me to ride. He can't find the axle nut. He had taken everything out of the car and scattered our belongings over the headstones creating a camper's quilt to keep the cold graves warm. Bicycle wheels, car wheels, bicycle parts, suitcases, books, dog food and dish, blankets, food, everything! I see him sitting on a black headstone holding his head in his hands. I could imagine the thoughts flying from his brain, "What in the world are we doing? This is the craziest idea Iris has ever came up with. How did I let her talk me into this? If this is what this trip is going to look like, we should just throw the bike and all our stuff into the car and go home."

I don't know what to say. I sit down beside him and put my head into my hands. We sit in silence until we both burst out laughing. Without saying a word, we put everything back into the car. He will drive back to Peninsula to either look for the parts in front of the Winking Lizard or buy new parts at the Century Bike shop next door. I will keep walking, this time downhill.

How will I keep my mind busy? I begin with a prayer for the first mile thanking God for my blessings and for the health and safety of my family and friends, for world leaders and the soldiers serving our country. After prayers, I stop and stretch. I do an abdominal exercise where I hold in my abdominals for a count of twenty and then breathe deeply for a count of ten. I continue this for about a mile. Then I enjoy the scenery and think about where we we'll have lunch.

Chapter Nine

Only the World

> God's red flaming sun
> sinking into rainbow sky.
> God saying goodnight.

Our first night on the road we eat dinner at a Texas Roadhouse. We walk outside just as the giant red ball sinks into the horizon. We hold hands and gaze as flames of red, orange, yellow, blue and purple explode into the burning sky. As we get in the car to drive to our motel, I look down on the floor and see something shiny, my "You can do it" pin!

> This morning I see
> sunflower trees. Their yellow
> petals wave at me.

On this cool, sunny day I walk into Medina, Ohio, which is only four miles down the road from our hotel. Jim finds Susan's Coffee and Tea where he drinks coffee and makes phone calls while he waits for me to arrive around lunch time. After sharing a sandwich in the park, Biscuit, Jim, and I walk around the square of this Western Reserve village window shopping in stores called Strictly Bears 'n Dolls, The Chocolate Box, Ormandy's Trains and Toys, Country Aire Gift Shop, and Logo's Bookstore where I buy five post cards. I see a Methodist church --time for a restroom break. I also want to leave a flyer about my walk and a letter from SPAN, Suicide Prevention Advocacy Network.

My thoughts turn to the people I've met in the suicide survivor community, especially to Elsie and Jerry Weyrauch, who founded SPAN, Suicide Prevention Advocacy Network. Their daughter Terry took her own life in 1987. Like most survivors, life as they knew it changed afterward. But they wanted to do something to prevent others from going through what they did. In 1996 they founded SPAN, a non-profit organization dedicated to the creation of an effective national suicide prevention strategy. This grassroots organization uses advocacy for suicide awareness, education, and prevention as its public policies. I remember attending that first National Suicide Awareness Day.

Journal Entry
May 10, 1996
Washington, D.C.
SPAN Walk

I am feeling anxious, like something wonderful is about to happen but also something painful. Much as I work to stay in the moment, my mind drifts. I see Eric, a smiling, mischievous little boy looking at me as if wondering what I am doing. I'm tying his tennis shoes. No, I'm lacing up the tennis shoes I'll be donating to a homeless man, donating them in Eric's memory.

More than two hundred people who have lost a loved one to suicide gather in Lafayette Park. We sing "Amazing Grace" and say a prayer of comfort, healing, and hope for the future. Pink, yellow, and green candles light our way as we walk through the park. New shoes our loved ones will never wear hang from our shoulders. I think about the homeless people who will benefit from our gifts. I recall the picture Eric took on his eighth grade field trip to Washington, D.C., a homeless man with all his possessions sleeping on the empty street. I always wondered what Eric was thinking when he took that picture. Now because of Eric, I'm giving shoes to another homeless man, shoes the size Eric wore, size 10.

As we walk in front of the White House we stop, hold our candles into the air, lost in our thoughts. Will someone hear our plea? Can we stop suicide? Can we stop our pain? As we walk around the park, the pile of shoes grows under a giant oak tree. My friend Sandy and I stop. We place our shoes on the top of the pile as we each say our son's name. "Eric." "Tony." We hug and continue walking. Our tears fuse with the raindrops falling on us now.

> Riding on the wind,
> Passing farms, woods, sleeping cows.
> Thank you God, for earth.

I've been biking this flat, empty road through cornfields for hours. My stomach starts growling and I'm feeling weak. I look for my wallet and realize I forgot to put it in my fanny pack. No restaurants but I pass country fruit and vegetable stands selling fresh tomatoes, melons, and green beans. No money, no snacks, just two bottles of warm water.

Around the bend, I see an oasis, a small country restaurant. I put my sales skills to work. Sales rule #1: Get the top decision maker. "May I please speak to the owner?" He's not in today. Next, ask for the manager, I'm talking to her. Sales rule #2: Be friendly. I say, "Sure is hot today." No response. Sales rule # 3: Get her attention. "I'm walking and biking from Ohio to Arizona," trying to impress her. I think it did.

Sales rule #4: Make your pitch. "I forgot to put money in my fanny pack this morning. But I could call my husband to get a credit card number to pay for lunch." No, their register requires the card to be swept through. Sales rule #5: Be polite but ask a question that can be answered with yes. I say, "Thank you. Could you please fill my water bottles with fresh ice water?" Sales rule # 6: Beg. I see two bananas on the shelf that should have been tossed last week. I ask, "Out of the kindness of your heart, could I please have one of those bananas?" She gives me an I-can't-believe-this-woman look and tosses me both bananas. I thank her and hurry outside. I sit at the picnic table devouring them as if I hadn't eaten in months. They taste like banana milkshakes I loved when I was ten. Rule # 7: Always have lunch money.

Clean white sheets waving
In the wind of memories,
Of days long gone by.

This mode of travel allows me to see the world close up and slowed down--things like clean clothes drying on backyard clotheslines, fields of Queen Anne's Lace, and advertising billboards. I see one enticing me to stop at the Ashley Place Tea Room and Gift Shop. It sounds so otherworldly I can't wait to explore its treasures. At the end of the day, before heading back to the hotel, we follow the signs to the tearoom. A quaint gift shop greets us with unusual gift items, china, knick-knacks, lotions, and, of course, tea. I find a treasure, bath salts. Not ordinary bath salts but bath salts from the Dead Sea. I can't wait to get back to the hotel to soak in a heavenly bath.

We establish a routine. After checking into a hotel we bring our things into the room. Jim sets up his computer and gets online. He takes care of work-related business, and then records the day's events on our website. Today it's my "begging for food" story. While he does his thing, I do mine. First ice for a cold glass of water and then I stretch. Most days my muscles ache so much I can't walk straight. I fill the bathtub with bubble bath and Epsom salts and soak for as long as the water stays hot. Tonight I use the Dead Sea Salts. As I soak and relax, my mind drifts back to my last pilgrimage. In January of 2000, I took a pilgrimage to the Holy Land. I think about the friends I made.

My roommate, Frieda, a Methodist minister from Missouri, became a good friend. I see the face of our guide, Shep, and remember his love for his God, his country, and his people. I remember the sights and sounds of that holiest of holy places, Jerusalem. I feel the salt water on my legs as I step into the Dead Sea. I wish I could have floated like the pictures I saw on the post cards in the gift shop, but the water was icy cold.

But I stood in it anyway letting the icy saltwater soothe my tired legs. As I walked out of the water, my feet and legs felt relaxed and light as tiny feathers. I thought about the place called Masada, a fortress built by Herod that sits on a cliff overlooking the Dead Sea, surrounded only by dessert.

I am so relaxed after my bath; I fall asleep and dream of floating on a sea of salt.

Masada
We drive slowly along the sea that is dead.
Sun slips into the sea or is it the sky, I cannot tell.
My tired eyes glare at the Rock.
Mountain- Fortress- Masada.
Herod's hiding place from the Jews.
Jews hiding from the Romans.
Romans hiding from the world.
We ride a sky car straight up in silence.
Our feet touch the same stones of those who built
Storehouses, baths, walking paths,
Palace, lookout tower, the room
Where the men drew lots to die.
We sit on synagogue sitting stones
Listening to our Rabbi Shep.
He speaks of his people and their love of God.
He speaks of his love for God,
Of man's responsibility to God,
Of God's responsibility to man.
On top of that fortress we break bread,

Drink from the cup and remember our own fortress.

Because the afternoons get hot, we try to get on the road as early as possible. This becomes my favorite time of day; just starting out, not knowing how far I will get or who I will meet. This country is nothing but farms for miles and miles, flat land, ideal for biking. I pass a field where a farmer is mowing a plant with little purple flowers that smell like grapes. Seeing a woman on a bike surprises him and he smiles. We wave like old neighbors who pass each other every day. Rolled haystacks dot the next field. I wish I could paint. Instead, I write a haiku.

> I love the smell of
> Summer. Early morning breeze,
> Rolled haystacks, heaven.

The morning is cool and overcast. I discover that nothing lies between West Salem and Ashland, Ohio. Nothing. So far I've had no difficulty in finding restrooms. I have a feeling today will be different. Few houses with giant front yards and long driveways line this road. No vacant lots or trees to hide behind. I do not want to find myself stooping in a patch of poison ivy. I'm getting desperate.

I start looking for a welcoming home, one I could walk up to the door and ask, "May I use your bathroom?" I find a two-story brick bungalow with a railing by the side door where I tie Biscuit. She is barking so loud I do not have to knock. An elderly woman comes to the door. By this time I have to pee so badly, I skip my lengthy explanation and just blurt out, "Hi, my name is Iris and I'm walking and biking from Ohio to Arizona. Please, could I use your bathroom? I promise to explain."

As I rattle out this sentence, the woman looks at the man and they both look at me. They see the desperation on my face and direct me to their bathroom. Returning to the kitchen relieved, I smell bacon cooking. I had interrupted their breakfast. I quickly relate my story and give them my letter that explains who I am and why I'm making this journey. They wish me luck as I hurry out the door.

Because I started so early, this day drags. I walk because the road is heavily trafficked with semi trucks that fly by fast and close to the berm, too close sometimes. My feet hurt and I'm getting a blister on my left middle toe. I have walked and biked through seven Ohio counties in six days. No wonder my feet hurt!

I walk into Ashland and decide to stop at Ashland College. I find the Student Affairs office located in the Administration building and talk to Shamar. She knows that suicide is the third leading cause of death in 15 - 24-year-olds which makes college students high-risk. I leave information about suicide prevention with her. She asks about Eric and I tell her about how he died. She hugs me and says, "You are honoring his life by traveling this journey."

I want to believe that. Recently I had a dream where we were living in the house on Bass Lake Road in Chardon. I was in the dining room singing,"In the jungle, the mighty jungle. the lion sleeps tonight." Eric came in and sang "A-wing, a-wang, a-wing, a-wang," and danced around the room. I said "My you sound happy today!" Then I woke up and remembered that Eric is dead. But maybe he is singing and maybe he is finally happy. And maybe it is true that I am honoring Eric's life.

> Biking down Rainbow
> Highway. Cool breeze on my face,
> Sweat down my strong back.

The days create their own rhythm. I ride in the morning enjoying the early coolness and quiet earth. As I travel west, the sun follows and the day grows warmer. I sometimes walk instead of biking just to catch my breath, cool off, and rest my butt. Today I ride on Rainbow Highway. Maybe if I follow it long enough I will reach the end of the rainbow and find my pot of gold.

I think back to the tenth grade when I had to write "a creative, imaginative speech." I had zero imagination or creativity. But I created an imaginary friend, a leprechaun who watched over me. For the first time in my life I felt good about myself. I was creative. Now I am creating a new life. Maybe the journey to the end of the rainbow begins on Rainbow Highway. Or maybe it begins with writing.

"I'm just another writer" writing my truth. My truth of who I was, who I am, and who I may be. I want to be in this present moment, this moment of discovering where I fit in this writing world if I fit in at all. Writing to heal a great pain, writing to understand someone, no not just someone, my own son who chose to die, chose to write a suicide note instead of a poem. A poem that might have healed him instead of words that killed him. I write to search for that answer, to search for my true and authentic self, to find the explorer in me who is ready to go "deeper and deeper into the world."

I find solace and wisdom in Ohio poet Mary Oliver's poem, "The Journey." It describes the "wild night" and the "melancholy I've journeyed through in the grief wilderness." My healing began when I read her words of going deeper into the world and saving the only person I could save-- myself. I could not save Eric.

I wonder if one day he plainly knew what he had to do. He did not listen or speak to anyone, he just did what he felt he had to do based on his twenty years of experience. He felt everything and everyone was against him. He was lost on that road and tangled in the "fallen branches and stones." He heard only his voice, which was "shouting bad advice." He "strode deeper and deeper" into himself instead of into the world to be consoled and guided by others. He was determined to save his life the only way he could. He was "determined to do the only thing he could do." Instead of saving his life, he ended it. Instead of ending my life, I am saving it by going "deeper and deeper into the world," into my world.

Now I am exploring this world, which makes me hot and tired. I'm close to Mansfield and decide to walk into town. We put the bike in the car and I grab my walking stick, shiny oak with a knot handle. I bought it in the Alps in Switzerland in 1998 when we traveled there for our second honeymoon. This fairyland country had been at the top of my "places to see" list since I saw a picture of icy mountain caps in *National Geographic*. The collection of colorful metal plaques decorating the top six inches of the stick remind me of the cities we visited, Grindelmald, Baden-Baden, Lucerne, Lugano, and our favorite, Zermatt, at the foot of the Matterhorn. I sat in the sunshine looking up at that giant, white-capped mountain and wrote a poem.

> On the rocks under the Matterhorn,
> Butterflies fly high on the mountain.
> They begin life as creeping, careful caterpillars, then
> Metamorphose into winged rainbows,
> And fly to heaven.
> What do they know that we do not?

Now instead of the mountains of Switzerland, I walk the hills of central Ohio carrying my walking stick and my memories.

I reach Mansfield's town square around noon where Jim and Biscuit wait for me by the fountain. We buy drinks and sandwiches to eat in the park. After lunch we explore the town square with its Civil War Monument and white band stand. We stop at the local NAMI office, the National Association for the Mentally Ill. I have a link to their website on my website and want to introduce myself. Jim stays outside with Biscuit. I meet Mary Kay and Darlene who tell me about The National Alliance for the Mentally Ill, founded in 1979. It provides support and advocacy for consumers, family, and friends of people with severe mental illness. This nonprofit, grassroots organization works to provide equitable services and treatment for the 15 million Americans living with mental illness. Local and state affiliates provide information, education, and support for funding, insurance, housing, rehabilitation, and jobs for people with any form of mental illness.

I say goodbye to Jim and Biscuit and start walking out of town. I walk and walk, losing track of time as the sun fries my brain. I'm hot, sweaty, and tired wanting to quit for the day, but I still have a couple of miles before meeting Jim at MailBoxes, Etc. where he's making copies of my letter. I see a sign advertising foot massages and reflexology. Maybe I could get something for my blister.

"May I help you?" the receptionist asks.

"I hope so," I respond. "I'm walking and biking from Ohio to Arizona in memory of my son, but I'm getting a blister on my middle toe. Do you have anything that would help?"

Silence, then, "Let me ask the owner. I'll be right back."

The owner of the shop, along with the other stylists and customers, listens to my story. She gives me some ointment and tea tree oil for my feet, at no charge. One hairdresser stops cutting her customer's hair and says, "I have to give you a hug."

"But I smell," I protest. She smiles. Another woman stops me at the door. "My mother completed suicide ten years ago and I still think of her every day. Thank you for what you are doing," As she hugs me, I think, "What am I doing?" and "How did I get here?" I'm too tired to think about it right now.

My toe hurts. I walked 7.5 miles and biked 8.5 miles, sixteen exhausting miles-- a good day. At MailBoxes, Etc.

Jim has found that the ink had run out on the copier. Since his office copier is the same and he's an expert at changing ink cartridges, he volunteered his services. A woman is waiting to use the copier. Jim says, "My wife is biking across the country and I'm her back-up man."

She responds, "You must be Iris's husband. She told me all about it. I commend you both for your courage." Mary Kay was from the NAMI office I visited earlier in the day. Jim was not surprised.

> Ride bike path today.
> Sweet smelling yellow angels
> Lead me on my way.

Today I ride my first bike path. This particular bike trail runs from Mansfield down through Bellville and on to Butler for a total of eighteen miles. It follows the former Baltimore & Ohio Railroad and is one of the many rail-to-trail paths that Ohio has created. I ride it from Mansfield to Lexington, a quick seven miles that brings me to the 100-mile mark! Jim gives me a congratulations card. Snoopy, flying along on his doghouse, says, "You did it with flying colors!"

I have not decided which I prefer, to walk or to ride my bike. My shadow keeps me company either way. I think of Henry David Thoreau walking around Walden Pond. His book, *Walking,* inspires me:

"The heavens of America appear infinitely higher, the sky bluer, the air fresher, the cold is intenser, the moon looks larger, the stars are brighter, the thunder is louder, the lightning is vivider, the wind is stronger, the rain is heavier, the mountains are higher, the rivers are longer, the forests are bigger, the plains broader."

Thoreau saw only a sliver of our country. I will see, really see, so much more: Ohio, Indiana, Illinois, Missouri, Oklahoma, the panhandle of Texas, New Mexico, and half of

Arizona. My heart is beating fast and I'm queasy. Can I really do this?

But look-- a Great Blue Heron. I love this bird's regal appearance. Seeing it soothes me: it has the ability to stand still, to be in one quiet moment, and then spread its giant wings and float away. When I am lucky enough to see one, I stand regal and erect like him and look into his eyes. The meaning of heron is "aggressive, self-determined, self-reliant, enables people to follow their own path, reflects aggressive movement toward opportunities that present themselves." An omen for me.

Blue Heron

I look for him in every pond.
Today I am lucky.
He stands still, tall;
His long neck stretched.
His grass-shadow mirrored in the water.
He bends down to scratch his neck
While listening to the duck quack him a story.
He looks around and takes soft steps,
"Spreads his wings--flying
to world I may never see."

Chapter Ten

Heart of America

Walking country roads,
Cars and trucks dart by,
Buggies go clippity-clack.

We are in Amish country. For every car that zooms by, two buggies trot down the road. I walk with Biscuit this morning. She barks at these "giant dogs" being ferocious. I see a young couple who look old. What kind of life do they have? I feel like a visitor from the future. They do not look at me as they pass. I wish I could stop and talk to them, but they are gone as quickly as they appeared.

The morning sun shines on a sea of goldenrod creating silky flags waving. The field is a yellow sea meeting the horizon and the solid-standing trees try to touch heaven. Heaven is what I am feeling right now. The not-awake sun makes the air cool. Butterflies flit from flower to flower as the light wind blows the goldenrod flags, creating waves that soothe me as I ride. I stop to take a picture, still now and soaking in the yellow field, the green horizon, and the azure summer sky. I smell the country; hay, cows, and a scent I do not recognize, clean fresh air. I listen; no birds singing, no human, not even a breeze. I am alone in this place, breathing in peace.

When I first thought of this journey, I envisioned people walking with me daily for a mile or two. Today is that day. I bike eighteen miles from Cardington to Delaware, arriving around 10:30 am. I find my friends waiting to walk with me through Delaware.

Anne and Pam drove down from Cleveland. Anne is my walking partner at home and we have walked and talked many miles. Janet and my eight-year-old goddaughter, Leah, drove from Reynoldsburg for this fun day. We walk and talk and laugh the three miles through downtown Delaware. Jim buys everyone lunch. We say good-bye to Anne and Pam. After a break we join the crowds to watch the All-American Horse Parade march through downtown Delaware.

I think about Janet and how she was my guardian angel those first days of my winter nightmare, a fog erasing my memory of any phone calls, family and friends gathering at the house, even Janet. She came to run errands, take care of details, and comfort me. I asked her to be my memory. Life has changed for both of us since January 1993. She now has two children and I have six grandchildren. We are both excited to be together sharing this day and being in this moment.

> Biscuit and I hike
> Down the loud road. Trucks fly by,
> Leaving cool breezes.

> Truckers honk and wave.
> "I wave back, wondering what
> Their lives are like now."

So many semi-trucks speed by, Biscuit and I move off the road, walking in the ditch. She is tired and wants to ride in the air-conditioned car with Jim. So do I. I see a sign, "Happy Wife, Happy Life." This wife is not happy; she is hot and tired.

In the distance, I see some kind of a business. Time for a potty break. I have my speech prepared and recite it to Lucinda, the receptionist at Select Sires. The air conditioning feels good. I ask, "Would you mind if I sit here and rest for a while?"

"Please do, you look hot and tired."

I tell her about my adventure and ask her, "What is Select Sires?"

"Our company collects and freezes bull semen and sends it to cattle breeders all over the world," she tells me. My philosophy: Learn something new every day.

> Sunflower soldiers
> Stand strong, straight at attention
> Praising Goddess Sun.

The temperature soars but the flat, open road makes the ride tolerable. I stop every two to three miles to rest in the shade. I pass a field of sunflowers, standing tall and still. Their stretched necks and solemn faces pray to their Goddess Sun. I stand, stretch my neck and raise my face to the Goddess Sun and say "Thank you, God, for this day."

I see a big shady oak tree and lie down under it. My bottom hurts, sweat runs down my back, legs, and temples. My entire body aches. But I have never felt so alive. At this moment I know I will complete this journey and it will change my life. Holding my camera at arm's length, I take a picture of myself to remember my 200th mile. Jim calls, "Meet me at a place called the Red Brick Tavern at the intersection of Rt. 42 and Rt. 40, only a few miles down the road."

By the time I arrive, I'm sweating so bad I can smell myself and it isn't White Shoulders. I walk into the cool air-conditioned haven. The dark room makes it impossible to see anything. As my eyes adjust to the darkness, I hear people clapping and shouting, "Hi, Iris, Jim's at the end of the bar waiting for you." He is talking to Larry, the town character who no longer works at the bar but thinks he still does. Larry disappears behind the bar to get me a much-needed glass of ice water.

Jim has been there long enough to tell everyone about our journey. Christy, the owner, wants to buy us lunch but I need a shower more than I need food. We'll come back for dinner.

At dinner, Christy tells us the history of the tavern, built in 1836 by Stanley and Ella Watson. The tavern was one of the first in operation when the National Road was completed through Lafayette. In 1859, it became the private residence of the oldest and only surviving son of Stanley and Ella. It remained in the family until 1912. It also served as a schoolhouse, tearoom, restaurant, and inn. Six presidents visited the Red Brick Tavern; John Tyler, Warren G. Harding, Martin Van Buren, John Quincy Adams, William Henry Harrison, and Zachary Taylor. Today the Fleet family owns and operates the restaurant, Ohio's second-oldest stagecoach stop. The Red Brick Tavern also gives rest, refreshment, and friendliness to pilgrims biking across the country.

> Geese fly overhead
> Sun asks me the question I
> Always dread, why, why?

The cloudless blue sky, bright sun, and cool air look and feel much like the day one year ago, September 11, 2001. As I bike Rt. 40, the National Road, heading towards Springfield, Ohio, I look down at the small flag inserted in my water bottle holder I've carried since the first day of this journey. Our friend Roger reminded me that we would be on the road on September 11th and thought I should carry a flag. With so many details in our planning, I forgot this one.

But the universe didn't. On that first day, walking alone for the first time, I stumbled on a stick with red cloth attached. I picked it up to find a small U.S. flag in perfect condition. Someone left it there just for me. Now as I stare at that flag I think about that day one year ago. I think about all the lives lost and the families left behind, people still in heavy grief. I ride in silence and pray for those thousands of families, sending them strength, courage and peace.

Journal Entry
September 11, 2001, 8:00 a.m.
Pinehurst, North Carolina

"What would life be like if we were awake in each moment? The World needs us, each of us. If we treated both ourselves and each other as if we truly believed that, would this world not be a better place?"
--Unknown

I love opening a new journal full of blank pages waiting for words that come from inside me wanting to be written, to discover through writing some new aspect of myself and my world. This journal is different from my others.

The tan leather cover is just that, a cover I can use over and over to cover a plain black journal. I bought it at Borders with the two birthday gift certificates I received from my two Lauras', my daughter and my step-daughter. When I write in this journal, I will think of how different they are but how both know me well enough to give me the same gift.

We came here to visit Jim's dad for a couple of months and rented a small condo on a golf course even though we do not play golf. I am sitting on our patio watching the golfers make their way to the 12th hole. The workers shut off the automatic sprinklers and left for the morning. It rained overnight but now the sun is peeking through the clouds. Last night we ate dinner on the patio, watching the lightning and listening to the thunder as it streaked closer. At times the sun sneaked through the clouds and shone on top of the tall pines like Christmas ornaments. The purple and pink sky seemed unreal, like a pristine dream that I did not want to end.

I woke this morning hearing enchanting music. Jim was on the computer trying to find words to a song, "I come from the land of the foggy, foggy dew, when walking in the morning is like walking through glue." We have a bet on which musical this song is played. He says *Brigadoon*; I say *The Princess and the Pea.* I know I'm right and plan to win my month of back rubs.

I finished reading Psalm 46 and want to remember verses 1-3: God is our refuge and strength, an ever present help in trouble. Therefore we will not fear, though the earth give way and the mountains fall into the heart of the sea, though its waters roar and foam and the mountains quake with their surging.

Jim is calling me into the house. Something is happening on TV. I'll write later.

How do I begin to write about today? For now, I can't. What I can do is walk. While I walk, I will scream, I will cry, and I will pray that our world is not ending.

> National Anthem,
> Flag flies half-mast. Kids plant tree,
> September 11.

Now one year later, I continue to walk and pray. My cell phone rings and startles me from my reverie. Jim has arrived in South Vienna, Ohio, where a community memorial is beginning shortly at the elementary school in the center of town. If I hurry, I can get there before it starts. For the next five miles, I peddle fast. As I approach the school, a woman holding the hand of a blond, curly-haired girl of about four sees me, "You must be Iris. Jim and Biscuit are over there waiting for you." I arrive in time to set up our folding chairs behind the lawn of children just as the ceremony begins.

A group of Boy and Cub Scouts circles the flagpole. The crowd is silent as one Scout in slow motion raises the Stars and Stripes and then lowers it again to half-mast. A young woman sings our National Anthem in a clear, strong gospel voice. We all stand to recite "The Pledge of Allegiance." The principal speaks of dates that defined past generations. He remembers his grandmother telling him about December 7, 1941, and America's headlong entry into WWII. His mother remembers November 22, 1963, and where she was the afternoon President Kennedy was assassinated in Dallas. He vividly remembers January 26, 1986, the day thousands of us watched television as the flames from the Challenger lit up the afternoon sky. And now, this generation will hold in its memory two planes crashing into two buildings now absent from New York City's skyline.

The ceremony continues as a student from each grade throws a shovel of dirt around the newly planted white pine. As the students return to their classrooms, each one stops and places into the ground the small flags they have been patiently holding. As the crowd of children shrinks, the field of flags around the pine expand.

> Red, white, and blue sea,
> Surrounds the tiny pine tree.
> We will not forget.

It's not even noon yet, still time to reach Springfield before the end of the day. A few miles down the road I see a lamp shop that draws me inside. Lamps and shades of all shapes and sizes fill the giant room. The next room looks like a glass rainbow filled with Tiffany lamps from floor to ceiling filling up every open space. I want to buy them all but maybe I can take a picture instead. What would I do with two hundred Tiffany lamps?

Donna asks, "May I help you?"

"No thanks, but may I take a picture?" I don't want the lamp police to arrest me.

I spend time telling Donna my story. She calls her co-worker, Karen, to meet me. As I repeat my story to Karen, I see her eyes tear up. Last year, her twenty-year-old son shot himself. Instead of going into the brain, the bullet came out through his mouth. He survived. Since then he's had two accidents and is still on drugs. Karen says he still grieves over his father's death. Karen still grieves for her son. We stand and hug for a long time.

I continue biking and say an extra-long prayer for Karen and her son. I wonder how many times in the past year she bargained with God. Did she promise to be good and never do anything bad again if only God would heal her son? I remember asking God to bring Eric back, to release me from my nightmare. I promised to go to church every Sunday, to tithe to the church every week, to be kind to everyone, to do whatever God asks. I promise, I promise, I promise.

But bargaining doesn't work. It didn't bring Eric back, and it won't heal Karen's son. It's just wishful thinking to get us through the nightmare. The truth is that we don't get through it; we live with it until we make a decision. Do we stay emotionally dead, dazed, depressed, and joyless, or do we do something -- like walk and bike across the country? Or like speaking about suicide to high school students? One day my friend Leslie called.

"Iris, I teach a class called Senior Seminar where the students have to present a community service project. I have three students who want to do their project on suicide and present a program called The Yellow Ribbon Project. Are you familiar with it?"

"Yes, I am. A couple in Colorado whose son completed suicide began it." I said.

"I told my students about you and they'd like to talk to you about helping them. Would you?"

"I would be honored. Leslie"

With the help of student volunteers, Gina, Erin, and Melissa created and presented an assembly to the entire student body. The Yellow Ribbon Project, sponsored by the Light of Life Foundation, helps prevent teen suicide by teaching them the warning signs, risk factors, coping strategies, and where and how to ask for help. They asked me to share my story. I realize that every time I talk about Eric and tell our story I heal a little more.

I shared a poem with them that I found in Eric's ski boot box where he saved cards, photos, notes from girlfriends and poems that I believe girls had given him. I do not know the name of this poem or who gave it to him but I hope it comforted him.

> If you should need
> Someone to talk to
> A shoulder to lean on
> I'll be there.
>
> And if you should need
> Time to yourself
> Your own space
> I'll step back
> To give you room.
> But you must realize
> That I need your help
> If I am to know
> Exactly what you need.

I continue riding until I reach the sidewalks just outside Springfield, Ohio, and then walk to meet Jim and Biscuit, who will walk with me through downtown. As I cross the intersection, I catch up with three women who look like they are returning to work from lunch. I tell them I am walking and biking to Phoenix and why. I love to see the expression on people's faces when I say this. One woman says, "You have to go to the television station and share your story. I'll take you there. It's just around the corner."

At the station we find a reporter, Cathy Stelzer, who grabs Bob, the photographer. She interviews me right outside the television station-- no lipstick, messy helmet hair, and sweaty bike pants. Bob films Biscuit and me walking around the town square.

We take Cathy's picture for our web page. She doesn't know when or if our interview will be televised because of the all-day coverage on the 9/11 anniversary. We thank her and continue our walk west out of Springfield.

> Morning sun on porch,
> Sipping coffee, breathing in
> Old and new memories.

I ride past a century-old home with a rainbow garden yard and ancient front porch. An elderly woman is sitting at her front window drinking coffee. We wave to each other.

It's sunny and warm and I feel like riding and riding all day. I ride from Springfield through Donnelsville, to Brant and on to Phonton. I've lived in Ohio most of my life yet I've never heard of these towns. I stop at a garage sale to look around and rest a little. I buy a pair of four-leaf-clover earrings and some scarves, small items I can carry in my bike pouch. I think about the people I've met along the way and make a point to write their names down so I will not forget them: Christy, Larry, Lucinda, Carol, Jason, Valerie, Mary Kay, Darlene, Karen. Who else will I meet on this adventure?

Chapter Eleven

I Turn to You

Leaving Ohio,
Entering Indiana,
The halfway mark, Yea!

Biscuit and I walk into Richmond, Indiana along Rt. 40, the National Road. I approach a park where I see a mammoth statue like the one I saw in Springfield, Ohio. A pioneer woman holds a baby in one arm and her other arm encircles a toddler who is clutching her skirt. I walk around the base and read the inscription:

NSDAR Memorial to the Pioneer Mothers of the Covered Wagon Days. Nation's Highway! Once a wilderness trail over which hardy Pioneers made their perilous way seeking new homes in the dense forest of the great northwest. The National Old Trails Road. The first toll gate in Indiana stood near this site on the National Road.

From a brochure I picked up at the visitor's center, I learn that the original idea for a National Road began in 1909 when a group of Missouri women wanted to locate the Old Santa Fe Trail. The idea for an ocean-to-ocean highway developed into plans designated by Congress as the National Old Trails Road. In 1911, the National Society Daughters of the American Revolution established a national committee to build the Old Trails Road into a great National Memorial Highway.

In 1924 the committee proposed a plan to erect twelve large markers designated as "The Madonna of the Trail," designed by sculptor August Leimbach of St. Louis, Missouri. This eighteen-foot-tall monument shows "The face of a mother strong in character, beauty and gentleness ...who realizes her responsibilities and trusts in God. It has a feeling of solidarity--a monument which will stand through the ages."

The Madonna I passed in Springfield was the first one and it was dedicated on July 4, 1928. The Richmond, Indiana Madonna was unveiled and dedicated October 28, 1928. In his dedication address, Harry S. Truman spoke of The National Road as "a long trail winding into the lands of my dreams to commemorate the memory of the Pioneer mothers who so bravely fought the hardships of covered wagon days to assist their men in blazing the trail that opened up the great Northwest to settlers, the autograph of the nation written across the face of a continent."

I felt awed and honored to stand before this inspiring monument. I could see the strength in her arms. But her face unnerved me. I could see her determination, strength, and trust, but her frank acceptance of the life she chose and the clear commitment to it were raw, speaking to me of sure tragedy to come for her. I thought about the hardships these pioneers endured to start a new life in an unknown land.

My little bicycle ride across the country on paved roads and resting at night in comfortable hotels along the way seemed insignificant. But I do feel like a pioneer moving slowly, with determination and acceptance into an unknown land. The Madonnas have motivated me anew.

As I continued walking the Madonna's face set in stone penetrated my mind and kept me company. Do I have her strong qualities? I was determined to graduate from college even though it took twenty-five years. I was determined to be a loving mother. I am determined to complete this journey just as I'm determined to make meaning of Eric's death and make a difference despite his loss and my loss.

I had the strength to survive a difficult childhood, so I expect that Eric knew I was a survivor and that I would survive this nightmare, which I trust is nearly over. I am both physically and mentally strong enough to keep going to the end of this journey and to continue the work that God has given me to do. I trust, too, that since he told me to make this pilgrimage, He will lead me to a safe completion. I trust Jim to take care of all the details. I trust myself to keep going.

I am coming to accept Eric's death, and to live with that acceptance every day. I accept this assignment God has given me. In my imagination I wrap my arms around my son and my daughter, walking despite tragedy towards healing and a new beginning.

> First rainy morning
> Then stormy, cloudy sky, cool,
> now hot sun returns.

Our first rainy morning allows us to sleep in and relax. By 9:00 a.m., the rain stops but still looks threatening. We are anxious to get on the road. We pack up the car, hop in, ready to drive to where I had stopped yesterday. We sit looking at each other trying to remember where that was, then realize that I ended right here at this hotel. Have we been on the road too long?

By early afternoon I walk eight miles and bike fourteen, through Old Cambridge, Centerville, Pennville, East Germantown, Cambridge City, Mt. Auburn, Dublin, Straughn, and into Lewistown. I feel like I'm on the moors of Great Britain rather than the hills of southern Indiana.

Jim is waiting for me at Susie's Antique Café. Its name disguises its décor, a Mexican restaurant lost in a time warp. Posters of cowboys from 1950's movies paste the rough blue plaster walls and Mexican bowls and baskets line the windowsills. Jim is sitting with Susie, the owner, who is eager to meet me. I just want to sit. I'm hot, sweaty, hungry and my rear end hurts. We ask her about the sign we saw coming into town.

One Light Festival
September 21
Food, Music, Crafts, Fun!

Susie explains that the state planned to remove the one traffic light in town but the village leaders protested and won. Now they celebrate with a "One Light Festival" every year.

After devouring the cheapest and best bacon, lettuce, and tomato sandwich I've ever eaten, I get on the road again. I want to ride another seven miles before the end of the day. The comfortable temperature and flat terrain help me achieve that. Another record-breaking day, walked ten miles, biked thirty-one! I made it to the halfway mark for this first phase, 336 miles! I compose a list of the "Top Ten Things I've Learned These First Three Hundred Miles":

10. A mile on foot or a bike is twice as long as a mile in a car.
9. Even with a padded bike seat, a gel seat, and padded bike pants, biking still is a pain in the behind.
8. There is nothing, No-Thing between Ashland and Mansfield, Ohio on Rt. 42.
7. The first mile in the morning is contemplative and goes by quickly, the 30th mile at the end of the day is a bear and takes forever!
6. Ohio has more cornfields and cows than tall buildings.
5. Heaven is a bubble bath, a back rub, and a bed.
4. Heaven is also a long, slow steady downhill road with a wide berm.
3. Hell is a long, steady uphill road with a narrow berm.

2. Love is having family and friends back home sending messages of encouragement and support.

And Number
1. The realization that I am married to the most gener-
   ous, understanding, loving, patient "Gem" of a guy.

> Cleveland, Sugar Creek,
> Philadelphia, I'm not
> sure what state I'm in.

I bike through these small towns until I reach the outskirts of Indianapolis where Jim is waiting. We put the bike
in the car as I plan to walk through the city and want to make
a few stops. First a jewelry store to repair my bracelet. I love
wearing jewelry and Jim has given me a collection of art
jewelry: earrings, necklaces, slides, and rings. For this trip I
wear only three pieces and my watch.

I'm wearing the tiny pearl earrings Eric gave me for my
birthday one year. The two bracelets I chose to wear remind
me of two special people. Zachary, my honoree when I
walked the marathon for leukemia, gave me a turquoise-
beaded bracelet that spells Health. The one that needs repair
is my Lifekeeper bracelet that my friend Sandy designed and
gave me. Since her son's death, she has dedicated her life to
suicide prevention and helping other survivors. The infinity
design came to her in a dream. She knew she had to create
this design into necklaces and bracelets for survivors to wear
to remind them to choose life.

I find a jewelry store just off the main street. The clerk
is a man about Jim's age, with thin gray hair and a slight
build. He looks tired.

I hold up my bracelet and ask, "Can you repair this?"

He looks at it before passing it to the repairman behind
the window.

"It's an unusual design. What does it mean?"

"It means infinity and is a symbol for keeping life. A friend of mine created the design after her son completed suicide. I am the survivor of my own son's suicide and I wear it to remind me that we are here to live and to remind others that life is a gift of infinite importance. I'm walking and biking across Indiana and the country in memory of my son who died nine years ago." He is quiet for a moment.

"My wife died recently and eight years ago my 29-year-old daughter completed suicide. I still think of them both every day."

He does not charge me for repairing my bracelet. We hug each other goodbye.

As I walk back to East Washington Street, I think about the jeweler and wonder if he ever talks about his wife's or daughter's deaths. Has he ever talked to a counselor or does he belong to a grief group? Men often keep their emotions inside because our society does not encourage them to feel or grieve openly: "I'm a man; I can do this without help from anyone."

A recent death brings back memories of a previous death, particularly if one did not allow oneself to grieve for the previous death. I experienced this when my grandfather died. At his graveside, I could not stop crying. Why? Then I realized I was not crying for him as he had lived a full life. I was grieving over the death of my grandmother who had died thirty years before. I had not grieved for my grandmother who had been more a mother to me. She died when I was nine years old and I did not get a chance to say good-bye. Instead of attending her funeral, I was shipped off to my cousin's other grandparents' house. I remember swinging in the back yard tree swing wondering when grandma and grandpa were coming to get me. They never did.

No one in the family told me where she was buried and I never asked, not until the day grandpa was buried. Why didn't I know that she lay under this sandstone-colored headstone, her name, Alma Myers, and her birth and death dates clearly chiseled there for eternity? Why didn't my mother tell me?

I've learned that grief is work, the hardest work we'll ever have to do in a lifetime. We do the work now or we do it later but we must do it. We have no grief teacher; we just stumble along and hope we make it through this nightmare. In my stumbling, I discovered Alan D. Wolfelt, author of *The Journey Through Grief, Reflections on Healing Grief.* To Wolfelt grief is our inward feelings and thoughts; mourning is the outward expression of them, our active participation in the grief journey. "We all grieve when someone we love dies, but if we are to heal, we must also mourn."

He adds that love and grief are alike: they both have the power to change our lives and we must surrender to both. To find meaning in the future, we must not forget our past: "For it is in listening to the music of the past that we can sing in the present and dance in the future."

Until Eric died, I knew little about myself. His death forced me to become acquainted with myself, to slow down and listen. I must ask myself: who am I? How am I changed by Eric's death? Where am I going? Why am I here? What is my purpose? How can I lead a more soul-centered life?

I've been asking these questions for nine years. As I answer them, I get acquainted with my new self; my soul celebrates being. Walking through woods, reading a good book, sitting quietly with my grandchildren or my friend, walking and biking across the country --all are times of retreat and rejuvenation.

Grief work is soul work. Death causes us to become more intimate with ourselves, with others, and with our world. This journey is the higher education of my soul, and has manifested so far in the unfolding of new ways of seeing my world. The people I've met have each instructed me in the way to go through them. I have discovered a new sense of direction and purpose in my life. I have reassessed my goals, reset my priorities, and become deeply connected to those I love.

Experiencing my grief is far more demanding than I ever imagined. Yet I have discovered I have the capacity to convert the pain into purposeful expressions by helping others. As I reach out to help others, I help myself and grow through my grief. But no mistake, it is hard work.

Chapter Twelve

Up from Under

> I stop to listen.
> Corn lightly restless in wind,
> Mozart's harpsichord.

I see a Borders Bookstore, a perfect place to sit and write to Helen in our Circle Journey Journal. We write to each other in a journal we mail back and forth, our way of keeping in touch after she moved to Florida in 2000.

September 17, 2002

Dear Helen,

I planned to write this journal-letter to you sitting under a big oak tree out in the middle of nowhere. I've been out in the middle of nowhere many times these past few weeks. But I'm writing in a place we both love, Borders having café mocha and a cinnamon scone. I think this building must have been a classic old bank in another life. Green marble columns, cherry wood and brass windows that say Discount, Collections Exchange and Passbooks transport me back in time. I feel strange to be in civilization.

I've enjoyed the solitude of walking and biking through this glorious country. Last week, I rode through Harmony Township, Ohio, where a couple of falling- down houses sit behind large oak trees that shade unkempt lawns. At the end of the only side street, the newly painted village church steeple reaches for heaven but also reminds me of the work that needs to be done here on earth.

I felt peaceful and happy, but guilty, too. Here I was enjoying this sunny day, this fine life, while so many others are still in their heavy, early grief. I sent prayers of strength, comfort and love.

Yesterday I was hot and tired. I found a shady oak tree and lay down under it. I felt like a kid dreaming away the summer. Time stood still over me, the tree, the sky, and the world. I thought how fortunate I am to have the support, the resources, the time, the energy, and the physical ability to make this pilgrimage. I talk with God every day, saying mostly, Thank You, Thank You.

I am amazed at how far I have come. Not only the last 370 miles of biking and walking, but the emotional miles through time that have brought me to this place of healing, wholeness, and peace. Thank you, dear friend, for accompanying me on this journey in spirit. Love, Iris

I restrain from purchasing a book I do not want to carry. I travel light. The rest of the day I walk through and out of Indianapolis, past the War Memorial Plaza, past the Museum of Art with the original "LOVE" sculpture by Robert Indiana, and past the Indianapolis Zoo.

Eating Animal Crackers
As I pass the zoo
Just ate a kangaroo.

Then heaven opens
Rain soaks and cools my body
Rainbow colors sky.

At last it rains. I
Stop to sing and dance before
Sun comes out again.

Rain, sun, rainbows, and people fill my days. I ride, stop for coffee or a meal in a local café, wait for the rain to stop, ride into and under a rainbow, then take the sun until it gets hot or it rains again. Between raindrops and rainbows, I talk to everyone I meet.

In Plainfield, I escape raindrops by shopping at Gaylan's, a sporting goods store. I found a couple of tops that didn't fit in my fanny pack. After dinner we return to pick them up. I tell the manager, Chad, about our journey.

"Wait here, I'll be right back," he says.

After a few minutes he returns, hands me a $10.00 gift certificate and says, "I want to contribute something for your cause."

I thank him and shop a few more minutes. I find the perfect item, a much-needed black sports bra. Thank you Chad and Gaylan's.

We have dinner at Chili's and chat with our waitress, Cindy. "I'll be walking by here tomorrow."

"Good! Will you please stop at my day job, Illuminations? It's a lamp and lighting place just across the street." With a name like that, how can I say no? The next day around lunchtime I arrive there to find Jim already waiting. We meet her co-workers Pam and Jody, and later Jim features them on tonight's website entry.

Next stop, Terre Haute, where I discover a bike path that takes me into downtown. I'm not sure where I am when I come off the path and neither is Jim. I do know I need to find a restroom, fast. No gas stations, no fields, so now I'm desperate. I walk into the local fire station. My having to pee is not an emergency to them. They point me in the direction of the bathroom and continue watching *Days of Our Lives*.

Finding a place to go to the bathroom is the most challenging activity of my days on the road. I bike another six miles but then rain falls, hard.

Before it pours, I see a sign, "House of Hope, Bible Training School." Surely they will let me use their bathroom. I am desperate. Why do I always wait till the last minute? I walk in and see a man and woman talking. I want to be polite and I wait for them to acknowledge me, but they keep talking. Finally I have to interrupt.

"My name is Iris and I'm riding my bike from Ohio to Arizona and I really, really need to use your restroom."

The man gives me the evil-eye look. "When I finish talking to this woman, I'll take you."

"You, don't understand, I need to go NOW!"

He gives me another look and says, "Follow me." He leads me through one dark room after another until we reach a door marked "Ladies." He waits silently and leads me back to the front lobby then continues his conversation with the woman. By now it's pouring and Jim calls to ask my location.

Trying to tell him where to find me is the second biggest challenge of the trip. After much negotiation, Jim realizes he is right across the street. The man and woman finally finish their conversation and she leaves.

"I'm sorry I interrupted you." I hand him my letter. Still he says nothing.

I see Jim pull up and run to the car. He asks "Is there a bathroom inside that I can use?" I laugh.

> Birds sing this morning,
> Church bells ring this morning. God,
> Thank You, for today.

Up to this point we have no trouble finding an acceptable motel. Our definition of acceptable is a clean room, hot water, coffee pot, working TV, AOL access, and dogs welcome. After traveling 465 miles we arrive in Greenup, Illinois. Forty miles from Effingham, Illinois, is home to a national Corvette show where over 4,000 Corvette owners converge annually for a weekend--this weekend. They buy, sell, and exhibit Corvettes and anything and everything having to do with Corvettes.

We find a Budget Host Motel in Greenup with one room left. The dark building in much need of a paint job surely looks budget, but we have no other options. A sign, NO DOGS ALLOWED, sits on the reception desk. The owner asks, "So do you all have a crate for that dog?" "Yes, sir!" In it we've stored food, extra coats, flashlights and all the books I knew I'd have time to read.

We unload everything from the crate. Biscuit will not get in it. Instead, she jumps on the bed and gets comfortable on top of the pillows just like every other night on the road. We have no AOL access, no e-mails, or website tonight. But we do have a roof over our heads.

Effingham sits in the middle of Illinois at the crossroads of Interstate Rt. 70 (east/west) and Interstate Rt. 57 (north/south.) I bike the service road of Rt. 70. As I approach the intersection I see a giant silver cross rising out of the ground and reaching into the clouds—what a shock and surprise so I stop to look. According to the brochures, "The Cross at the Crossroads," 198 feet tall, is a symbol of hope and love for the 50,000 people who see it each day as they travel through the middle of our country. "It shines both in the sunlight and the darkness to remind travelers of God's love." As I pass it I say a prayer.

> Full white La Luna
> Shines with early morning sun,
> Slowly disappears.

I feel as if I am the only person on the planet as I ride my bike in the early morning with the full moon to keep me company. I have difficulty keeping my mind and eyes on the road because I am spellbound by that moon and my memories of July 20, 1969, when the entire world was glued to a TV. The human man walked on that "white mystery Man in the Moon." I was living in Spain, pregnant with my daughter. We did not own a television, so we went outside to look up at the moon. We pretended we could see Neil Armstrong taking those historic first steps.

> As I look at the stars near dawn,
> The silver sliver of the moon
> Slides across the sky.
> Stars beam silently
> Crying sheets of tears
> That tumble round our fears
> Till the sun decides to shine.

Just as every day is a surprise, so are the nights. The Corvette show ended and the 4,000 people went home, leaving us our choice of motel rooms. After last night's motel, Jim splurges and books a luxury suite in Effingham. Splurging means a Jacuzzi next to the bed, a room overlooking the indoor pool with hot tub and sauna, and easy acceptance of dogs. We do sacrifice AOL. Ah, a night alone with Jim minus his computer! That's really splurging.

> Wooly bear, squiggly
> bear crossing the road. Do be
> careful as you go.

Today I start early enough to see the sun rise. I am not a morning person, so this is a special treat and a great accomplishment. It's so cold, I wear my long pants for the first time. The road is smooth and absent of traffic. The only traveler I see is a brown wooly bear slowly crossing the road. I bike eight miles before I meet Jim at the National Road Café where we chow down eggs, sausage, toast, and coffee. We vow to eat more breakfasts together and see more sunrises.

We travel through Illinois's covered- bridge country and often stop to take pictures of old bridges, newly constructed bridges, and the green Illinois countryside. It sprinkles and then sunshine comes down again. Birds sing, church bells ring--reminding me it's Sunday. I ride through Martinsville, Jeavett, Woodbury, and Montrose. It's getting hot, but I bike forty-one miles before 1:00 pm. Early start means early finish.

Yellow, blue, orange, white
Butterflies roam tall golden
Grasses, pure delight.

I have now walked or biked over four hundred miles. Along the way I've seen many roadside crosses. Some are plain white with a name painted on the front. Others are adorned with real or plastic flowers, flags, stones, candles, angels, and teddy bears. Sometimes two or three crosses keep each other company. I remember the last day I was in Phoenix after Alec was born, the day I placed a cross next to a dirt road in the desert where Eric ended his life.

So many crosses
Line the road, names, dates, flowers,
Lives ended too soon.

I'd been reading *Women Who Run With Wolves*, by Clarissa Pinkola Estes, Ph.D. around the time Alec was born in February of 1995. Estes describes *descansos's,* resting places in the form of crosses placed along the roadside to indicate a death happened here, someone's life journey ended. "Right there, right on that spot, someone's journey in life halted unexpectedly," she explains. These crosses, these places must be remembered and blessed. Estes adds, "*Descansos* mark the death site but also note our suffering. They are transformative. There is a lot to be said for pinning them down so they don't follow us around, a lot to be said for laying them to rest." I saw it was time for me to remember and bless this place in hopes that it would transform my grief into something I do not yet know. At Home Depot, in Phoenix, I purchased two pieces of pine and twine to make a cross. On the horizontal piece I painted Eric's full name in purple. On it, I placed a grapevine wreath with yellow silk flowers, two red carnations from the bouquet my husband sent me for Valentine's Day and a special bouquet.

Before I left, I also wanted to climb a mesa. My daughter's friend Laurie called to ask if I would like to climb Usury Pass with her. I invited her to help me plant my *descansos* and then we could climb the mesa.

The day was typical for an Arizona winter, sunny and warm. We drove south out of Phoenix. In one moment, the city stopped and the desert started. We drove to the spot described on Eric's death certificate. It was greener than I remembered. I hammered the descansos into the ground and snapped a picture with my camera. Laurie walked away leaving me alone with Eric in my thoughts. I wrote him a letter in my journal.

February 15, 1995

Dear Eric,

I'm here, close to where you chose to leave this earth. I can feel you as I sit with the hot sun on my back. I see you in the ducks swimming on the pond next to this lonely dirt road. I hear you in the song of an unfamiliar bird singing just for us. Oh, Eric, I miss you. I brought you a descansos I made myself. The purple iris is from me, the white carnation from Laura, and the yellow sunflowers are from your newborn nephew, Alec. I wish you could hold him.

You picked a peaceful place to end your not-so-peaceful life. Cattails grow on the edge of the pond, the only sound is that of birds chirping, and the dirt road seems to go nowhere. How did you find this place in the dead of night? I like to think that the stars were shining down on you, especially Orion. Maybe he gave you some comfort. He comforted me the night I thought of dying. Perhaps he held out his sword in hand to welcome you to heaven. I hope you are now at peace. Thank you, my dear son, for your love and laughter. I love you and miss you. Love, Mom

When Laurie returned, we said a prayer and then said good-bye to Eric. Instead of driving to Usury Pass, we found a mesa just down the road. As we hiked up the path, I picked up two stones and a piece of dried cactus. Laurie explained the Native American tradition: "If you take something from the desert, you must leave something behind." I removed a barrette from my hair and clipped it to a small bush. We looked up the trail and saw a jeep at the top coming down the mesa towards us. We moved to the side for it to pass. The two men in the jeep stopped. A smiling brown face looked at us and asked, "Would you two young ladies like a ride down the mesa?"

"No, thank you," we replied. "We're going to the top." As they drove away, we laughed. I had never been picked up on a mesa before; of course this was the first mesa I'd climbed.

The desert was beginning to bloom with deep, tiny, yellow flowers; purple and yellow barrel cactus; and giant saguaros spreading their arms. The sun shone on the distant mountains and an owl flew overhead. I remembered the song I sang in my fifth- grade choir concert. "God's in his heaven, all's right with the world."

The setting sun suggested that it was time to head down the mesa and home. We passed dairy farms, orchards, vineyards, and cotton fields. As we drove towards the city, the sky to the east darkened to a blue-black, and we could see the rain pelting down in the distance. To the west, the sunset swiped the sky with yellows, pinks, golds, blues, and purples, a picture only God could paint. Directly above us hung two of the brightest, clearest, deepest-colored rainbows I had ever seen. We stopped to look at the sky. Slowly the rainbows disappeared; the sun set and only black sky remained. As the Earth and Sky danced, I felt God say, "Life does go on."

Yesterday's rainbows
Finger-paint on evening sun.
Earth dances with sky.

Chapter Thirteen

To Make You Feel My Love

> Bumpty-bump road
> My body jiggle-jaggles,
> Then smooth road, comfort.

Up to this point I've traveled paved roads with little traffic. Just outside of Greenville, the road is being prepared for resurfacing. The surface is bumpy, deeply grooved, rough, and dirty. I pray this ends soon but it keeps going on and on. I call Jim.

"How far am I from town?"

"Just a few miles," he replies.

By the time I meet him at Applebee's my body shakes, my legs wobble, and my bottom hurts. I can't sit down. I can't stand up. But I have miles to bike before I sleep.

After lunch I bike to Pocahontas where I stop at an antique shop to pee and rest. I gaze at the knick-knacks, old pictures, and antique bottles, furniture, and dresses. A group of older ladies sit in rocking chairs facing a fake fireplace. I picture them drinking tea and discussing the day's events from another time and another life. It is shopping day and one by one they pay for their purchases and file out to the waiting bus returning them to the present.

I find a bracelet, an embroidered handkerchief and a serving tray with flowered tiles. I ask Betty, the owner, if I can return for them later when my husband picks me up in the car.

"Out for a bike ride?" She asks.

"Not quite."

We share our stories. Her son has been on Ritalin for three years, and he's more depressed than before he started taking it. He tried to hang himself when he was twelve, but the light fixture broke and thankfully he did not succeed. He is doing better today but still fights depression. Betty asks if she may give me a hug. We mothers cling to each other sharing our grief.

I expected to be having conversations about suicide and grief with people I met. In addition to sharing my story, I wanted to put something comforting in people's hands to get them through the dark night of the soul. In response to September 11, the National Association of Poetry Therapy published an anthology of poetry, *Giving Sorrow Words, Poems of Strength and Solace*. This little book of poetry is a gift to those in grief and sorrow and can only be given away. I read a poem and place a copy in her hands.

Hope

Hope
is the belief
that one hand
reaching to another
can eventually
touch the moon,
allowing the light
to guide us
through the night.

--Nicholas Mazza.

After leaving the antique shop, I bike along the National Highway, almost like a bike path here. I think about Betty and her son and say a prayer for them.

My ringing phone brings me back to the present. Jim wants to know my location. I can't hear him because I am next to Interstate Rt. 70 with noisy semi-trucks flying by at eighty miles an hour. I can't tell him where I am and we can't hear each other. We talk at the same time, while our frustration with each other grows. Our second breakdown in communication, not bad for traveling over five hundred miles in less than a month. We find each other and silently return to the antique shop to pick up my purchases.

> My last day biking.
> Next stop St. Louis. I will
> Enjoy trail's end--now.

A cool, clear morning but different, September 26, 2002, is my last day on this first phase of my journey. An easy ride, little traffic, flat smooth road until I reach Rt. 40. I'm coming into the Collinsville, Illinois, business strip; heavy traffic without a berm or sidewalks makes this hazardous. Jim gave me directions to Main Street where I find him sitting on a park bench waiting for me as he has every day this past month. He has become an expert on where and how to wait for me.

Collinsville is another town where time has stood still. I find the township office building where I use the restroom and ask for a lunch recommendation. The clerk directs me to Tommy's just down the street. Jim and I share the daily special; two Sloppy Joes, applesauce, chips and two drinks. I haven't eaten a Sloppy Joe in years and it tastes like the ones my grandma made. When our check arrives, we think it is a mistake, $4.00. Good--and cheap too!

We want to get as close to St. Louis as possible today. As I bike out of town I grow excited. I still cannot believe I've walked and biked almost six hundred miles! I ride past the Cahokia Mounds, a park filled with children climbing on green hills. I learn that the Cahokia Mounds is a 2,200-acre historic site that preserves the remains of the largest pre-Columbian city north of Mexico. It holds over sixty mounds including the one- hundred-foot-high Monk's Mound.

I want to stop but I want to get to St. Louis more. Just after I pass the park, I see a giant silver rainbow in the distance. It's the Gateway Arch of St. Louis. The sun sparkles on the silver making it look like angels' wings taking flight.

I think about my real angel who came the day Eric died, my sister Rose. That night I called my mother to tell her Eric died. I heard her scream. Then a calm familiar voice came on the line.

All Rose said was, "We're on our way."

I had forgotten that she, her husband, John, and their eleven-year-old son, Bobby, had returned to the States after being stationed in Germany for the previous four years. They arrived in chaos and for the next week quietly took care of our day-to-day needs. One morning my nephew Bobby asked if I'd like to take a walk. He held my hand and listened to me cry as I told him about Eric, the cousin he would never know.

Many years after my heavy grief, Rose and I talked about how that day affected her. Bobby was her second son. Her first son, William Carl, died the day he was born. She later wrote a letter to share her feelings and emotions of that week with me.

July 10, 1999

Dear Iris,

We've talked about some of this but you may have forgotten so I want to put it in writing for you.

As you know, since the death of my son, God has allowed me the privilege to minister to other mothers who

132

have faced the death of a child. I never thought that twelve years later my own sister would need ministering to.

We just returned from a four-year tour of duty in Germany where John was stationed in the Army. Many things happened in those four years. John was deployed to the Gulf War, his father and brother died, we lost an adoptive child, and in January, 1993 we were returning to the States and beginning again at a new place, Ft. Drum, in upstate New York. And just in time.

We arrived at our mom's and my dad's house, exhausted and ready to relax a few days before reporting to our new location. We asked Mom about you but she thought you were still in Florida. The phone rang and I was surprised to hear it was you. Mom could not understand what you were saying as you were crying. I heard you say, "Eric is dead." I told you, "We're on our way."

I remember when we talked about William's death; I sensed you did not fully understand how I could grieve so long for him. William died the day he was born. I never got to see him take his first step, say his first word, or watch him go off to school. Even though I had him for but a brief moment, I mourned him for many years.

I counseled mothers who lost newborns, yet how would I be able to help you? You had Eric for twenty years. You saw him through his childhood to become a fine young man. He had, in your eyes, so much to look forward to in life. Yet in one quick decision, he was gone.

I wondered if it took me so long to grieve William, how long would it be before you would not have that same feeling of despair and loss. All I could do is show you the Love of God. That God will take care of us in good times and bad. In *Hebrew's* 13:5, God reassures us that, "I will never leave thee, nor forsake thee." We do not understand why we have to go through this pain and suffering. Our instincts tell us: "I can't handle this! It's too much! It's overwhelming!" But

God says with his still small voice, "Honey, you're my child and I love you. I will take care of you."

I know that God helped both of us when our sons died. And now he uses us to minister to others. God says in *Romans* 8:28, "And we know that all things work together for good to them that love God, to them who are called according to his purpose." God has worked together for good in the death of our sons. Always remember that. Love, Rose

Now I look at that silver arch-angel and thank Rose for her love, support, and healing words. I know she is right. We minister to help others heal, and in that healing we are also healed.

I bike another 32 miles before we reach the edge of the city. Our plan was for me to keep biking until we reached sidewalks. Jim would park the car and he, Biscuit, and I would walk across the bridge to the arch. We had not thought about how we would get back to the car with the dog. As I pass the city limits sign for East St. Louis, I start to get nervous. I'm not a city girl and this one doesn't look friendly.

Jim calls to say, "Wherever you are, stay there. I'm coming back to pick you up."

A minute later we have the bike in the car and head back to Collinsville. We decide not to walk into the city for safety reasons. But we're at St. Louis the end of the first phase of our trip, of our pilgrimage!

From our hotel window just outside of Collinsville, we see the arch again. After resting, showering, and reading e-mails, it's time to see St. Louis, the Jefferson National Park and its Gateway Arch. The sun shines on the arch making it look like half a giant golden ring circling the earth. We stand for a long time just looking at it, then take a walk around the park with Biscuit. A woman jogging stops and asks, "What kind of dog do you have? I have an Australian breed of dog that looks just like her."

We say, "She is Shepherd-Beagle." Then I say, "This park is grand, you must enjoy having it in your city."

"Oh, I don't live here. I come here once a month for my job. This is my first time in the park. I live in Lakewood Ohio, a suburb of Cleveland."

We tell her we're from Aurora, Ohio, and explain how we arrived here and why.

She says, "I'm proud to say that I'm from the same area as the two of you. You must be proud of what you've accomplished." I say a silent prayer as we continue walking.

Dear God,

Thank you for bringing us safely to the end of this first phase of our Arizona journey, to end in this glorious city of St. Louis. Thank you for the challenges you gave Jim and me to bring us closer together if that was possible. Thank you for guiding us, for being with us, for listening to me and helping me hear you. Thank you for our friends and family who were with us in spirit and tracked our progress on our website and encouraged us with notes and e-mails. Thank you for our grandchildren and godchildren who were our inspiration. Be with us in this transition between traveling and being home again. Please give me the courage to write my story to share with others who may need its message. I know this is my purpose and you have given me the talent, skills, and the time to do it. Thank you for all these blessings. Amen.

> God's sun shone when we
> Began our journey. It shines
> When we reach this end.

Chapter Fourteen

Make a Change

October 1, 2002

Dear Eric,

A warm, sunny day and your grave called me to visit. I feel comforted when I see your name and the dates you lived. I don't have to tell you about my journey because you were with me every step, every mile, every day. Thank you for being my guide along with God and Jim.

I gained strength, confidence, discipline, and a belief in myself that I never knew I owned. Every day I concentrated on the road for safety and mindfulness. I prayed, wrote haiku, and memorized poetry. I met people who shared their stories of grief, loss, and healing with me.

Jim and I worked as a team. We discovered that we could be together 24/7 yet still talk to and love each other. I could not have done this without him. As we said in our marriage vows, we are partners and are now a great team. Oh, we did have our moments of conflict but they passed as quickly as they came. I also had moments when I asked myself, "Can I do this, will I succeed?

But every day I got up, got dressed, and got on the road with no other thought than, "What will this day bring?" I kept going, and before I knew it, 26 days and 613 miles evaporated. Diane asked me how I felt being home. "Strange, I don't think I've processed the experience yet. It's going to take me a few days, maybe weeks or years to figure out what it means."

Physically, I'm stronger and in better shape than I've ever been in my adult life. Emotionally and mentally, I feel whole and healthy for the first time since you died. I feel I can do anything I choose to do and that includes writing a book about this experience. I must tell our story.

I want to continue the process I began as I walked and biked; praying, eating healthy food, talking to strangers, walking, biking, and smiling. I like the way I look and feel right now which is not 54. Your mom is changing and growing. I think you would like who I am now and it's all because of you. I wish you were physically with me.

I wonder what you would be like today at age 30 and what you would be doing. Are you married, do you have children, do you still make people laugh? You would have been a good father and uncle. You missed so much these past ten years. But you are with me always. I love you, Mom

Journal Entry
November 21, 2002

Give thanks for this day
Made perfect in its own way
My dead son's birthday.

Dear Eric,

Happy Birthday, Eric! It's your 30th birthday! The ninth birthday without you on this earth. I still find it difficult to comprehend, to understand, to believe that I am living without you. I still miss you so much. I celebrated this birthday differently from all the others since you've been gone.

Do you remember our last Christmas together? I still replay the conversation we had as we drove to find the perfect tree. You weren't excited and I said, "You know how much I love Christmas and always try to make it special for you and your sister. When I'm dead you'll think about this day and feel bad because you didn't enjoy it more." You responded, "Mom, I'll probably die before you and I'll probably be shot." A sliver of fear ran through me. I didn't know how to respond and laughed it off as a dark joke.

Were you trying to tell me something you had been thinking about, and I didn't listen? I regret not asking more questions but I regret many things. If we had talked, would you still be alive?

When you were little, you loved Christmas. I think you still liked it but thought you needed to be too manly to admit it. Together we brought the tree into the house. You strung the lights like your dad always did. You hung the ornaments you made in grade school-- the shiny balls with your name in sparkles, the sled out of Popsicle sticks. I placed the twirlies that belonged to your great-grandmother close to lights so they would spin. I found a place for the red and green crochet trees and the plastic icicles I made for our first tree. The decorated tree was perfect for a perfect Christmas. Two weeks after this joyful, blessed Christmas, you were dead. How long will I ask, "What if...?" I miss you so much. Love, Mom

The tree still stood in the front window the night the policeman came. It had to come down but I could not look at it or touch it. Laura and her dad arrived late on Saturday night. They helped Jim un-decorate the tree and stuff the ornaments and decorations into boxes that have been stored in the garage cupboards until today.

I am now ready to open them. I purchased two green artificial wreaths, some ribbon and wire. I wanted to create memory wreaths, one for Laura and one for me. I invited Diane to help as I didn't think I could finish this project alone. I opened the box and stared at the newspaper dated Saturday, January 9, 1993. I felt a tear on my cheek as I unwrapped the paper to find a green and purple glass ball that Diane immediately recognized. She gave it to me that Christmas, 1992, and I had forgotten about it. Out came the shiny balls with Eric's and Laura's names with the date

1978; the popsicle sled Eric made in first grade, two brass ornaments with both names on them and great-grandmother's twirlies. We placed them on the dining room table and stared at the array of colors, shapes and sizes, a legacy quilt of ornaments.

I could not go on. Luckily Biscuit had to go out. Diane continued working. I didn't know if I could face this painful past. As I walked Biscuit, I thought back to September when I walked through Ohio, Indiana, and Illinois. Then I looked to the months ahead when I would be walking to Phoenix. If I can walk across the country, I can face these memories.

When I returned, Diane was busy placing the ornament with Eric's name on the wreath she was making for Laura. I said, "I invite you to help me and here you do all the work!"

"This isn't work, this is fun, Iris." I began working and then realized that it *was* fun. I hung my wreath on the brick wall above the mantle. I looked at it and thought of Eric. My friend Marsha McGregor wrote this poem for me.

Ten Years After
For Iris

A decade later
I am brave enough
to open up this box
and see the treasures there
along side the pain.

I pull back the tissues
oh so gently
like bandages
and let the light in.

They are still intact
well preserved and waiting for me.
I celebrate their history,

their simple joy.
They tell a story
of you
and me
and our time together
before and after.

I've kept them safe all this time
let that wound stay covered till it healed.
Today it is ready
I am ready
to give it sunshine and air.

With this unwrapping
I celebrate two birthdays:
yours and another Son
both humbly born
both cherished by their mothers
both grieved deeply
but forever alive.
You are both a part of my Christmas.
Let the angels sing.

--Marsha McGregor

Journal Entry
January 7, 2003

Dear Eric,

I woke early today and watched it get light outside. I can't say I saw the sunrise as it's going to be another dark and cold day. I started a fire in the fireplace and looked out at the foot of snow on the patio table. It stopped snowing but it's cold, 10 degrees.

It's also ten years since you died. I feel like time stood still for me and sped ahead for everyone around me but I know this is not true. I have moved forward little by little, especially this past fall when I started my pilgrimage. I have to keep reminding myself that I too am moving forward into my future, healing, changing, and growing.

What do they say? "Life goes on." I look at Laura and see her life now. Married with three children in these ten short years. She tells stories about you to keep you alive in their lives and in her life. They know you loved Halloween, driving your car, music, doing tricks on your bicycle, and playing jokes on your friends.

My mind is racing faster than I can write. Jim asked me what he always asks me on this day, "Would you like me to stay home with you today?" I always answer the same, "No." I made it through nine of these days, I can make it through another one. I took down "the box." It's an old ski-boot box where you kept all the notes and cards from your friends, especially Beth. I read a couple.

I cannot read them all though, and I can't throw them away. I'll think of something to do with them someday. I looked at pictures of you as a cute little boy. I read the journal you had to write in the 2nd and 3rd grades. "It was fun," seemed to be your favorite sentence. I hope you had fun when you were little.

When did you stop having fun? Was it when your father and I divorced?

Many years ago Laura shared a conversation the two of you had on your 13th birthday, the day before your dad and I divorced.

Laura said, "Today's your birthday! Bet you can't guess what you're getting."

Eric asked, "What?"

"Guess?"

"The trip to the Bahamas with Jamie that I asked for a couple weeks ago?"

"In your dreams, guess again."

"The new bike I've been wanting?"

"No, guess again."

"Oh, come on, just tell me."

"Something you never dreamed you'd get. We'll you're not getting it exactly, Mom and Dad are."

"What are you talking about?"

"Mom and Dad are getting a divorce, that's what I'm talking about."

Laura said your face turned white and you stomped out of the room.

Oh, Eric, I was in so much pain at the time I couldn't think of anyone else's pain, not even yours or Laura's. Was our divorce the catalyst that began your roller coaster life and moved you toward your final decision? Another question I cannot answer. Another thought I've had in my mind these past ten years. Another forgiveness I've worked towards. Please forgive me as I work on forgiving myself. Love, Mom

Journal Entry
March 21, 2003

I am so tired. For the past two months I have worked on my CPT homework, presenting poetry programs at several nursing homes, and taking a class at Kent State called "Teaching Poetry in the Schools." In addition to attending the class, I've been teaching poetry at a grade school, a high school and a nursing home. In between I get in some walking and exercise classes at the gym. I've also presented a journal-writing workshop at the library and several suicide-prevention talks at local high schools. It feels so good just to sit here at the airport resting and writing in my journal.

I'm on my way to visit Laura and the kids. She called yesterday from the doctor's office, crying. She had a miscarriage and saw the fetus. A nurse came in and stroked Laura's hair and just let her cry. I should have been with her. She's had so many experiences in her short life; I want to help make her pain go away. I will hold her in my arms and let her cry as long as necessary. For now I will cry for her.

I will also cry for our country. Yesterday we went to war with Iraq. I couldn't write about this yesterday and still is difficult today. I see people getting on planes to Phoenix, to Newark, to Dallas, to wherever. And now thousands of our sons, daughters, husbands, wives, sisters, and brothers are going to a country on the other side of the world, a country most Americans can't even locate on a map. Our president sent them to fight a war for what? To free Iraq, to end a regime ruled by a monster, to finish what his own father started twelve years ago, to retaliate against terrorists, to lower the price of oil, to guard the oil, to keep from blowing up our world? I do not know, does anyone? All I can do is pray and write a poem.

I Know

I know I should but cannot
Watch T.V. fouled with tanks and troops
And bombs falling on people we do not know.

I know I should but cannot
Read the paper showing a smiling face of a boy-soldier
Or a woman who sacrificed her body and soul.

I know I should but cannot
Breathe, my stomach in knots, the lump of fear stuck in my throat keeping me from speaking a truth.

I know I should but cannot. I will just pray.

Chapter Fifteen

High Powered Love

May 30, 2003: The Second Phase Begins

> While on a journey;
> My dreams wander
> Over a withered moor.
> --Matsuo Basho (1644-1694)

Car trouble delayed our departure. The air conditioning compressor broke and where we're going we'll need air conditioning. But we're on the road again, driving to St. Louis, Missouri, to begin the second phase of our journey. As we drive along Rt. 40 where I biked last September, memories prepare me for what lies ahead. I am as nervous as I was that first day but for a different reason.

I've been so busy since the beginning of the year that I haven't had time to get back into shape. I've walked every day but just enough to exercise Biscuit. No time for weight training or long bike rides or even long walks.

"When was the last time you were on your bike?" Jim asks.

"Do you want the truth or should I lie?"

"How about a lie?"

"Oh, just the other day,"

The truth is I have not been on my bike since the day I rode into East St. Louis last September. Thinking about beginning this new phase and what lies ahead makes me tired. I sleep until we reach the outskirts of Indianapolis where we plan to spend the night.

We eat dinner at a Red Lobster. Halfway through my clams, I remember Red Lobster was Eric's favorite restaurant. He loved clams! Every year our neighborhood gathered together for a clam bake, an all-day festival of eating, drinking and playing. As young as four, Eric was the only kid in the neighborhood who ate clams, two to three dozen at a time. Every year on his birthday we went to Red Lobster where he'd get embarrassed when we sang "Happy Birthday" to him.

One year I talked him into trying lobster. He discovered he loved it more than clams. The first birthday after his death, we took his two best friends, Gabe and Rob, to Red Lobster to celebrate Eric's 21 birthday. We toasted him with his favorite beer, Miller Genuine Draft, and told him how much we missed him. Now we sit in another Red Lobster in another city drinking a toast to him and still missing him.

Sitting next to us is a family of mom, dad, two girls, and a boy. The waitress brings out a candled cake and sets it in front of the mom. They sing "Happy Birthday" so quietly that when the song reaches the end they are almost whispering. I don't know if they were embarrassed or just a quiet family. Without thinking I jump up and sprint to their table and Jim follows me for fun.

"Excuse me, but I think you can sing 'Happy Birthday' to your mother better than that. Now let's try it again."

I lead them in another round, this time singing at the top of our lungs. Everyone stops eating to listen. They are so surprised all they can do is say, "Thank you." We return to our table and continue our meal. As they leave, the older girl, Shelby, stops at our table. "Thank you for helping us sing 'Happy Birthday' to my mom the way we should sing it. We couldn't decide between Red Lobster or Olive Garden. I'm glad we came here." We were glad too.

In one instant, rain
Stops, Sun shines, God smiles.
Reminds me it's time.

It is strange driving through the towns and country I walked and biked last September: Richmond, Brazil, Terre Haute, Effingham, Marshall, St. Elmo, Pocahontas, and Collinsville. Tomorrow I will be walking through St. Louis and collecting new names and memories. It is raining so hard that we don't see the arch until it is right in front of us. In one moment, the rain stops and the sun shines. God is welcoming us back to this city.

We drive the route I plan to walk tomorrow, Rt. 40, but soon realize it's the industrial section of the city, not picturesque. Jim revises the route, taking me through downtown, Forest Park, and by the zoo, more appealing to my senses.

Mary Kay and her family live in Des Peres, a suburb of St. Louis. Mary Kay is a friend of my friend Shannon, and I have not seen her in many years. Shannon told her about our journey. We did spend time with her last September before we headed home. She invited us to stay with her and her husband, Dave and their daughter, Sarah, when we returned for the second phase. We promised we would.

A couple of weeks ago I called to tell her when we'd be back in town. Surprise, she and Sarah would be visiting her brother in California and she was not sure when she would return. But Dave, whom we've never met, insisted that we stay with him. We arrive before Dave but the cleaning lady lets us in. Before we could bring our bags in, a UPS truck pulls into the driveway. Jim says, "That's for me." Just before we left he ordered a wireless connection for his computer. His secretary shipped it here. He is so excited. Now he'll be connected to his office every day as long as we're in an area with a signal. When he's connected, he's happy.

Early morning wind
Blows sweetly as I continue
My healing journey.

I start walking from the arch. The day is cloudy and windy so I take off my hat to keep it from blowing away. It looks like it could rain any minute but never does. By the end of the day the sun is shining. I approach a neighborhood where a group of people are standing on the sidewalks holding signs in front of a dark brick building. It is Planned Parenthood and they are picketing against abortion. A woman hands me a pamphlet and I give her my letter and tell her why I'm walking.

"May I give you a hug?" She asks.

As we hug, I stare into a picture of a fetus and a shiver runs down my back.

I continue walking but she runs after me. "Your middle name is Llewellyn? I know someone by that name. Are you by any chance related to Steve Llewellyn?

"No, Llewellyn is my first married name. I kept it as a connection to my children. And I know my ex-husband has no relatives living in St. Louis." Another woman and a little boy came up to me and hands me a bouquet of red carnations. I thank him and continue on. I say a prayer thanking God that I never had to make that decision and a prayer for those who did.

I walk through Forest Park, the location of the 1904 World's Fair. A policeman rides by on a horse and we wave to each other and smile. I see a group of people wearing familiar purple shirts. It's a Team-in-Training for Leukemia and Lymphoma group who are training for the Anchorage, Alaska, marathon scheduled in a couple of weeks. This is their twenty-mile day. I tell them I was a member of a Team-in-Training and walked a marathon in Cleveland two years ago. I show them my Team-in-Training pin on my cap. They

147

give me a high five as I continue on. After walking another five miles, Jim brings me my bike. I ride ten miles into Des Peres to Dave and Mary Kay's house. First day, twenty miles and I'm not tired.

> Yellow finch, blue jay,
> Red cardinal, robin redbreast.
> God's feathered rainbow.

McDonald's and I have become great friends. Every city corner and small town has one with clean restrooms. Biscuit and I walk about two miles when we see the familiar arches. I am wearing my cap with a picture button of Eric on the front and my pink t-shirt with his name and the date of his death on it. A man approaches me and introduces himself as John. "Who is Eric? He asks.

"Eric is my son and I am walking and biking from his birthplace in northeast Ohio to where he died, Phoenix, Arizona. You can travel with us on our website." I hand him our letter. The family at the next table listens, too. As we talk, John takes out his wallet and says, "I don't have a lot of money but I want to make a donation to your cause."

"We are not taking donations," Jim replies, "but financing this journey with our own funds. We do encourage you to donate to your local mental health agency though or look on our website for a number of suicide organizations that would appreciate your donation. They need funds for suicide education, awareness, and prevention. That's the only way we can stop this epidemic." As we say good-bye, he shakes our hands and says, "I am proud to know you."

> Rain, rain today. I
> Rest, relax, read poetry.
> God, thank you for rain.

Our sunny weather ends, now rain, rain, rain. If it's sprinkling, I bike until it begins to pour when I'll meet Jim at a local diner for coffee, food, or soft drinks, depending on the time of day. While I bike, my mind races with my body. I need to exercise my mind. I memorize the Prayer of St. Francis of Assisi.

Lord, make me an instrument of your peace.
Where there is hatred, let me sow love;
Where there is injury, pardon;
Where there is doubt, faith;
Where there is despair, hope;
Where there is darkness, light;
Where there is sadness, joy.
O Divine Master, grant that I may not so much
Seek to be consoled, as to console;
To be understood, as to understand;
To be loved, as to love;
For it is in the forgiving that we receive;
It is in the pardoning that we are pardoned;
And it is in the dying that we are born to eternal life.

The cool, cloudy days roll into one another as I bike through the Ozark foothills. Here, I should say, I bike down the hills and walk my bike up the hills, up and down all day. Between the hills and the raindrops, we enjoy the eclectic Missouri cuisine. We nestle in the Hen's Nest Café drinking fifty-cent cups of coffee. As Jim works on his laptop, the waitress asks, "Is that a laptop computer? I've never seen one." Jim shows her some pictures and an e-mail he just received.

In Sullivan, we enjoy a home-cooked meal at the White House Grill, meatloaf and mashed potatoes. In Cuba, we fall in love with smoked beef at "Hicks" Bar-B-Q King, "The Ozarks finest smoked." We pass through St. James too early in the day to visit its winery, but Joe's Diner, an old-fashioned 50's diner, entices us to try their giant hamburger.

I stop at the local bookstore, The Book Addict, for a children's poetry book and *The Right Words at the Right Time,* by Marlo Thomas. I take a few minutes and open to the middle of the book and read Paul McCartney's story. He was going through a difficult time when he had a dream about his mother who had died twelve years before. He could clearly see her face and especially her eyes when she gently told him to "Let it be," to keep going and everything will all work out. Talk about finding the right words at the right time! Thank you, Marlo and Paul.

As we head west, I am thankful for the cool, cloudy days as the terrain changes from hilly to miniature mountains. I coast downhill, standing to give my backside a rest. Uphill I test myself to see how far I can ride to the next tree or bush or sign and then get off and walk the bike to the top and do it again. I admire this part of the country I have never seen before and pray that I will reach the summit soon.

I say an extra prayer when I see the long, gradual downhill resting slope. I think about the sorrow that has walked with me these past ten years and what I have learned from each step. I memorize an untitled poem by Robert Browning Hamilton:

I walked a mile with Pleasure.
She chattered all the way,
But left me none the wiser
For all she had to say.

I walked a mile with Sorrow
And n'er a word said she
But oh, the things I learned from her
When Sorrow walked with me.

Grief is the hardest work I've ever done and it doesn't seem to end. My friend Iris Bolton lost her son to suicide in 1977. She describes grief like climbing a mountain in Peru on her South American pilgrimage, when it was difficult to keep going, she stopped and rested for a while. She called on God and her friends for help. After resting and praying, she kept climbing until she reached the top. On our grief journey, we also take a few steps, rest for a while, ask God and friends for help, and keep going. I keep going.

Sweet honeysuckle
Teases me. Blue indigo
Sweeps across my path.

Some towns like Doolittle are just dots on the map. Others are small metropolitan areas like St. Roberts home of the Army base, Ft. Leonardwood. We have lunch at Jack's Rt. 66 Diner, a back-in-time-diner with good food and a friendly waitress, Penny. On the back of our bill, she writes a note with a smiley face. "Safe journey! What a woman!"

Here we begin to see remnants of Rt. 66, Main St. U.S.A. I will be traveling this relic of a road all the way into Arizona. Most of Rt. 66 is either the service road of Interstate Rt. 44 or no road as it winds through small towns. Some have created scenes of the Rt. 66 of yesterday: Rt. 66 signs, cafes, museums, and unique visions pertaining to Main St. USA. Others are ghost towns with one gas station and two or three houses that look as if they could fall down any minute.

Through Missouri, Rt. 66, nicknamed "Bloody 66," follows the ridges and valleys which twist and turn making for dangerous stretches of highway and deadly accidents. In 1956, Congress passed the Interstate Highway Act, constructing faster and safer highways across America that ended the glory days of Rt. 66.

As I ride along
I hear birds sing this song,
"Welcome to our world."

Despite the rain and because of the cool temperatures, I'm averaging about thirty miles a day. An article in the local paper states that "Missouri is experiencing the rainiest and coolest first week of June they've had in a long time. This is unusual for us, don't you just love it? Yes, I do. Most mornings it rains, then gets cloudy in the afternoon but by the end of the day the sun shines and it's hot and muggy.

Today is that kind of day. I stop at one of the little dots on the map, Buckhorn. By the time I meet Jim at the Texaco station, one of the two businesses in Buckhorn, I am so hot and tired all I want to do is sit in the air-conditioned store and drink cold, cold water. As I park my bike next to the brick wall, a woman approaches me and asks, "How far did you bike today?"

"Thirty-one miles today but I started in St. Louis six days ago. And last September I biked from Ohio to St. Louis."

She congratulates me and introduces herself. Debbie says, "I'm a long distance bicyclist and I know how difficult and fun it is." But when I tell her why I'm biking, she begins to cry.

"I'm afraid my daughter may try to harm herself and I don't know what to do. I'm estranged from her. Will you say a prayer for me and my daughter?"

"Yes, I will." I add both to my daily prayer list. We exchange gifts. She gives me a tape of hymns and I give her a copy of *Giving Sorrow Words*. We hug for a long time. She does not care that I smell sweaty.

Early morning rain,
New friends share stories, tell jokes,
Royal golden sunset.

Jim has been waiting for me inside the Texaco long enough to make friends with Wes and Sam. Jim shows them his card trick and they share jokes, each trying to outdo the other. Sam, who is eighty-one married his first wife in 1948 and kept her for sixteen years before trading her in on a nineteen-year-old. Then he remarried his first wife in 1988. Jim says, "I've been married three times. Iris is Number Three and the last." We all laugh so hard. We'll return in the morning to start from here.

In the downpour the next morning, we check out of the hotel and hope the rain stops before we get to Buckhorn. It does not, so we sit at the Texaco station for two hours meeting other locals as they come in to have coffee and visit. Wes introduces us around. A giant man comes in and introduces himself as Tony but everyone calls him Bear.

"What is your name, Tony or Bear?"

With his Missouri grin and gleaming eyes he tells me, "My name is Bear but I don't tell strangers that until they become friends." Then he adds, "Ya know, they say I was born a beautiful baby--but this ugly was beat into me. Have you ever met a real hillbilly? Well, you have now!"

We could spend the entire day here laughing and talking with these charming Missouri folk. But our sides ache, our faces hurt from laughing, and the rain has stopped. We say goodbye and get back on the road.

From Buckhorn to Lebanon the road winds, climbs, and disappears in places. It dead-ends by a bridge under construction. We see a creek, a path, and a construction worker in the distance. Jim asks him if a bike could get through. "It's possible but you may have to walk it, as there's only a dirt path." Decision time, I either follow the path about a half mile up to the road or go back to the highway and come all the way around. I choose to walk the dirt path but Jim definitely has to drive around, about 20 miles.

I'm nervous. The path looks so secluded--how many construction workers are around? But I kiss Jim goodbye, then walk across the narrow creek and up the path. At a fork in the path I go right which takes me back onto the highway. Oops. I turn around and retrace my steps to the other path. I whistle, sing, and pray until I reach the road. Now I have to pee. I look around and see only woods. My mind conjures snakes and poison ivy. I see a shack with a sign for, "Sam's Stone and Gravel Co." Maybe I can use their bathroom.

I reach the door and call out to see if anyone is around. A tall, shaggy man peeks through the rusted screen. I give him my "walking/biking from Ohio to Arizona" speech and ask if I can use his restroom.

His face twitches into a smile and he says, "Sure can, but it ain't purty."

"It's better than the woods, isn't it?" He leads me from one dirty room, into an even dirtier one until we reach the bathroom. I close the door, look around, afraid to move. Black stone dust covers every inch of the floor, the walls, the ceiling. The tub is red rust instead of porcelain white. The toilet has black crud inside and out. Ugh! I stand still for a minute before peeing, thinking maybe I should go back into the woods. I thank him and hop on my bike. Thank goodness I carry Wet Ones with me!

The sun is shining when I arrive in Lebanon. It's still early even though I biked twenty-five miles. Jim suggests the three of us walk through town so I can get in a few more miles. We walk four miles. Jim gets a blister, Biscuit gets tired, and I can keep walking. As rainy as the morning began, the day ends with a golden sunset.

> Blue heron swooping
> Low along the winding creek
> Looking for his lunch.

Sometimes I go for miles without seeing another human being. I am so excited then to meet up with Jim, to have someone to talk with. The birds keep me company on the road and I try to find them in the branches to discover what kind of bird is singing to me. My rear end hurts from riding twenty miles to the outskirts of Springfield, Missouri, so I walk for a while. I think the spirits are sending messages to friends back home that it's a good time to call. I talk to Diane and Shannon for the next six miles. Both are following us on the website but wanted to talk to me to make sure I'm all right. It's good to hear their voices reassuring me that I'm not crazy.

Springfield, Missouri -- a "big-little" town -- is our first real experience of traveling back in time to when Rt. 66 was the only route across America. We find a Best Western named the Rail Haven. Built in 1938, its name "Rail Haven" originated from the split-rail fence that surrounded the cottages. Three rooms are decorated to honor Marilyn Monroe, James Dean, and Elvis Presley. We stay in the Marilyn Monroe room with 1950's décor, a large Jacuzzi, and floor-to-ceiling mirrors. Biscuit loves it as much as we do.

> White cotton-ball clouds
> Leading me West, whistling winds
> Want to slow me down.

Downtown I approach the Daily Record building of the local newspaper. I need a break from the hot sun. I introduce myself to Beverly, who tells me this is not the daily newspaper but a legal publications office. I tell her my story and she insists that I do go to the real newspaper, *The News Leader*, a couple of blocks away. She gives me a reporter's name, adding "I just know he'll want to write a story about you!" After walking in circles in the hot sun, I find the newspaper office and ask the receptionist, "May I speak to Steve, please?"

"What's it about?"

I tell her and she relays it to Steve on the phone. Evidently, he's not interested in writing a story about some crazy lady walking and biking across the country.

But the cool air conditioning feels good. I am not ready to go out into the sun and I need to pee. I see a sign, "No Public Restrooms," but that certainly could not mean me. I ask the receptionist if she could make an exception for an over-fifty-year-old woman who is walking and biking across the country. She cannot.

"Thank you," I politely say and leave.

> Sun shining as I
> Ride along Sunshine Highway.
> Road names bring memories.

I pass Iris Drive, then Violet Drive. I wonder if I'll see Rose Drive. Then down the road, I pass Rosehill Drive, close enough. I like to tell my name story: I'm Iris, my mother is Violet, and my sister is Rose. However, when my daughter was born, I did not want to give her a flower name. She was born while I was stationed in Spain in the Air Force.

When the nurse brought her to me she said, "What a beautiful baby! What is her name?"

"We named her Laura."

The nurse, from the Basque area of northern Spain, told me that in her language, "Laura" means flower. Now I have a step-daughter Laura and I discover it's also the name of a grandmother I never knew. Life is full of irony—and flowers.

The town of Aurora is off my biking route but we decide to drive through it at the end of the day. Since we live in Aurora, Ohio, we thought we should see what Aurora, Missouri, looks like. Smaller than our Aurora and the local newspaper is *The Aurora Advertiser*, where as ours is the *Aurora Advocate*. But both publish local-interest stories and local advertising.

We stop at the paper and introduce ourselves to the reporter, Judy, and tell her we are from Aurora, Ohio, and what we're doing. Judy spends time listening to our story and takes several pictures. We find out several weeks later that the paper did publish the article, "Mother walks across states to remember her son."

> White feathers along
> The road keeps me company
> As I creep along

The wind is wicked. It's sprinkling and the hills are killing me. I look for the downgrades and say a prayer of thanks as I fly down the tiny hills giving my bottom a rest. Today I hit the three-hundred-mile mark though we've only been on the road eleven days. I'm finding white feathers along the road and stop to pick one up. They remind me of Hansel and Gretel leaving the bread crumbs along the path in the woods so they can find their way home. They keep me company as I ride along. I smile when I see one and know that I'm heading in the right direction, forward, thinking more about the future instead of the past.

I wonder how this healing journey will change me. What will my life be like when I finish, not just this second phase, but when I reach Phoenix? Will I be a different person and what will be my next journey? I found a book called *The Art of Pilgrimage, The Seeker's Guide to Making Travel Sacred* by Phil Cousineau. He says that, "Pilgrimage is a transformative journey to a sacred center, a spiritual exercise, an act of devotion to find a source of healing, risk, and renewal. A journey without challenge has no meaning; one without purpose has no soul. This kind of journeying moves us from mindless to mindfulness, soulless to soulful travel."

I have been on a healing pilgrimage for the past ten years, and I now add the physical pilgrimage. I know I am a different person since the day Eric died. The way I choose to live today is a result of Eric's choice to die. I want to make meaning of his life and of his death.

I Wish

I wish my first poem was not about death.
Of watching a brown box being lowered into the ground
With the body of a boy who chose not to become a man.

I wish my first poem was about a butterfly in my garden,
A royal Monarch, resting on a purple petunia.
Spreading her wind-wings and choosing to fly.

--February, 2003

My thoughts are interrupted as I see what looks like the picture on the postcard I bought yesterday--a field of round orange flowers, Indian paintbrush and castillejas, which bloom from May to July on the prairies of Missouri. Then I see a rainbow-yard of wildflowers: pink cosmos, giant yellow sunflowers, white yarrow, wild zinnia, and others I've never seen before and don't recognize. I wish I could paint!

Instead I write a prayer.

Dear, God, you sure did make this world colorful!
You made Missouri hilly!
Please help me up this hill!
Please let there be a downhill grade soon!
Please let there be a place for me to pee soon!

Dear God, my rear end hurts!

I ride into Monett, our last town in Missouri. I'm meeting Jim at Ernie's Grill for lunch. Before I find the place, I stop to talk to Ed and Wendie who are riding their Cushman Motor Scooters on Missouri's Rt. 66. Ed gives me his Cushman Club of America card. Printed on the back is, "Thou shalt not love thy Cushman more than thy Spouse and Children; as much but not more." Ah, the colorful people we meet! We have traveled Rt. 66 from St. Louis to almost the southwestern edge of Missouri. I wonder what Rt. 66 in Oklahoma has in store for us. We'll find out tomorrow.

Chapter Sixteen

There Must Be an Angel

Moisture on my face
Tears mix with raindrops as my
Thoughts turn to Eric.

We cross into Oklahoma at Miami, home of six Native American tribes: Miami, Modoc, Ottawa, Peoria, Seneca-Cayuga, and Shawnee. This morning we have to drive twenty minutes to the place where we ended yesterday. It stopped raining before we left and now it's simply cloudy and cool. After only three miles, rain again, so Jim finds Michael's Family Diner where we have a hearty breakfast: eggs, sausage, toast, and coffee. By the time we finish, it stops raining and I'm back on the road, Rt. 60 for a while instead of Rt. 66. The lightly traveled road makes an easy ride into Seneca. I have been on and off Rt. 60 as it stops and starts. No road signs make it difficult to know if I'm still on the right road. I see a man working in his yard. I ask him, "Am I still on Old Rt. 60?"

"Yes, you are," he reassures me. "How far are you biking?"

"To Phoenix, Arizona,"

"Wow!"

As I tell him why, his eyes mist up. He tells me that several years ago his three-year-old granddaughter died in a car accident. "She was the only one wearing a seat belt. I think about her every day and I wonder if the day will come when I can think of her without crying."

"One sweet day," I tell him.

As it begins to sprinkle, I start to cry and my tears mingle with raindrops.

Eric has been with me in spirit every day and especially since I've been on this journey. I hear him say,"Keep going, Mom, you're doing the right thing. I am so proud of you." I biked and walked from Ohio to St. Louis last September and now I've biked across Missouri and yet I still can't believe that I'm doing it. I must be crazy. Then I hear his voice, "No, you're not, Mom. You're doing exactly what God told you to do for me. And for us together."

In *Conversations with God Book 3,* by Neale Donald Walsch, I learned that God does talk to us in a small voice within us and all we have to do is listen. To be who I am I must listen to God. This means following up and doing what the voice, God, tells me. Not do but be that person. One who puts into action what one hears from the heart. That is who I am.

On the day Eric died, I met John K. who reminded me of the Serenity Prayer by Reinhold Neibuhr:

"God grant me the serenity to accept the things I cannot change, the courage to change what I can, and the wisdom to know the difference."

Recognizing what we can change enhances the piece of control we believe we've lost: at these times, the perception of losing control becomes our reality. We feel we have very little control over anything. As a result, we must look for small things we can do to overcome our sense of powerlessness, even though these actions may not bear fruit immediately. The key is to do something. We can't change the bad situation, but we can do something to change our response to it and we can just physically 'do' something: clean out the kitchen junk drawer, volunteer at a nursing home; deliver healthful food to the local food bank. That's a start.

I have been doing little something's like walking, writing in my journal, and writing poetry. These activities helped me heal by learning more about myself, so I can accept myself. When I tell Eric's story, I heal a little more. Today I am more helper than griever. Now Eric reminds me that I am doing what God told me to do, to walk in his memory and to keep going.

As I bike into Seneca, I notice the green, spring-fresh countryside with gently rolling hills. The sun is high and it's getting hot. I've biked thirty-five miles, the most miles I've ridden per day on this phase. Command central, Jim's code name, calls it a day.

> Two blue herons there.
> One stands stone-still on the creek,
> The other dances.

I cross over the Neosho River and stop to look down the riverbank. Alongside the creek, I see a blue heron standing so still it could be a statue. I stand still for a long time waiting for it to fly away. It doesn't. But another one swoops so low into the creek, I can almost touch it. I watch it seem to dance on the water.

Sometimes when I walk, I look down to see if anything interesting is on the ground. I've seen: a brown sandal, Rolling Rock beer bottle, Coke, Sprite Ginger Ale, Orange Crush pop cans, candy wrappers, underwear, rags, shoes, a shirt, a piece of carpet, and gloves. I've also seen Queen Anne's lace, buttercups, and rainbow fields of wildflowers. I picked up a red silk carnation that I keep in my journey journal. I've also picked up: bolts, spoons, forks, pennies, nickels, quarters, feathers, a piece of rubber with hooks on each end, and stones. Today I find a white one in the shape of a heart.

> Mother cow watch as
> Calves run and jump and have fun
> In the summer sun.

I see my first snake, a skinny, slithery thing that skitters away from me as fast as I run from it. I wish my grandson Joey, the family's snake and bug lover, had given me lessons on snakes. He could have described poisonous ones to me and told me how to keep from getting bitten. I add the request of not seeing a snake to my daily prayer list. I am in farm country and pass fields of horses, cows, bulls, goats, and even llamas.

> Bulls watch me go by,
> I wonder if they wish they
> Could run free like me.

In addition to the heat, we run into road problems. Parts of Rt. 66 no longer exist, Rt. 60 is heavily trafficked, and Interstate Rt. 44 is out of the question. Jim opens his map program to find an alternate route. He finds a red dirt path of up and down hills with no traffic, no houses, no civilization. Earlier in the day in Vinita, we did experience real civilization, a Starbuck's. Well, almost. The Skylight Bakery and Café, in a historic hotel with a grand ballroom, offers a limited selection of Starbuck's coffee. Oh, it tasted heavenly.

Vinita is also the home of the World's Largest McDonald's, which spans Rt. 44, called the Will Roger's Turnpike from here to Oklahoma City. This McDonald's is a distinct Oklahoma landmark and should not, really could not be missed.

> Two dogs follow me,
> Big white Fred and little Brownie,
> My guardian angels.

Now I'm on a dirt road walking my bike up the steep hills, keeping to the middle of the road as I watch for snakes to come slithering out from the bushes. Again I wonder "What am I doing here?" Just then I see that two dogs are following me. Both mutts are so friendly they didn't make a sound. I name the big white one Fred and the scraggy one Brownie. They walk with me and keep me company for miles. Just as quickly as they appeared, they disappear. They must have been guardian angels protecting me from snakes.

We see a sign for the 57th Will Rogers Stampede PRCA Rodeo, The Rodeo of the Year tonight in Claremore, hometown of Will Rogers.

Jim asks, "Hey, hon', do you want to go to a rodeo? It's something we've never seen."

"I'd love to but please get comfortable seats. My backside hurts."

Jim splurges on box seats in the front row. Box seats, we discover, are hard folding chairs instead of hard benches. Thank goodness I brought my comfy pillow as the seats are hard, hard, hard.

We plunge into the excitement of our first rodeo. A parade of horses with riders decorated in red, white, and blue carry U.S. flags and gallop around the arena. Following them all the "little cowpokes" bounce up and down on their broomstick ponies donated by the local Wal-Mart. I want to grab a broomstick to join them in their fun. My favorites are the bronco riders who try to stay on the bull as long as possible. And I think *my* butt hurts!

Clown cowboys run around the ring picking up hats, debris, and thrown-off riders. Constant motion forces our eyes and ears to pay attention as we don't want to miss what's going on. We meet Anita, Don, and Laurie, rodeo experts who try to explain the rules but we are laughing hard and making so much noise we cannot hear or concentrate. We relax and enjoy the show.

Then Don looks at us closely. I had on jeans, white t-shirt, a chunky fake-stone necklace, and a straw cowboy hat, to cover my messy hair, I looked like a local. Jim wears a white Izod shirt, a blue fishing hat, and his brown deck shoes, a preppy from the East. What are we doing together?

The next day the road to Catoosa is difficult and dangerous. Jim has to drive me across two bridges, as neither has sidewalk or berm. Back on my bike I pass the Blue Whale, one of the many icons along Rt. 66. A giant blue whale sits on a little pond that was once a swimming hole but is now just a surprise along the road for tourists to stare at and wonder what it was like here in the olden days.

Then this part of Rt. 66 becomes the entrance ramp for Interstate Rt. 44, which I bike in terror for what seems like miles. A speeding truck can easily hit me. By the time I reach the QT station where Jim is waiting, I am shaking so hard I have to sit down. Jim had been visiting with a Girl Scout troop washing cars to raise funds for their troop. I am happy to just sit and rest for a while. The girls all pet Biscuit who is enjoying the attention. We take pictures and give them key chains with our website that we have been passing out. Hugs all around.

Now I'm back on the road headed toward Tulsa, twenty-five miles today and four hundred miles to date.

> Hot sun scorches me
> Sweat beads running down my back
> Not even noon yet

I write a chant today.

My Thanksgiving Chant.

Morning sun, I thank you.
Evening moon, I thank you.
Rolling hills and meadows,
Trees that touch the sky.
Clouds floating high.
Birds sing lullabies.

God all around me,
God inside of me.
Namaste, I thank you.
Namaste, I thank you.

Tulsa is a great biking city but I also have a near-death accident here. I am riding the business strip into town, not paying attention to the traffic. I get off my bike at the light to cross the street but I don't wait for the WALK light. As a result a car in the left turning lane almost hits me. I come so close to the car I can almost touch the front bumper. I scream, breathless as I cross the street. After turning, the driver honks at me, I'm sure calling me names. I don't think I'll tell Jim.

Jim finds a bike trail next to Riverside Drive, which runs along the Arkansas River. A covered bridge crosses the river as the path continues on the other side. I see a man taking pictures. I park my bike and approach him. "Would you please take my picture?" The shocked look on his face tells me he thought I wanted him to take my picture with his camera. I quickly grab my camera from my fanny pack and ask him again.

Don smiles and takes my picture. "How far are you biking today?" he asks.

"I'm walking and biking to Phoenix. I left St. Louis fifteen days ago. But I did phase one last September from northeast Ohio to St. Louis."

Then I tell him why. He introduces me to his wife, Sharon, and their daughter, Sandy whose wedding they're in town to attend.

"I would be honored if I could take your picture with my camera, too." Before we say good-bye, I give them our website. A couple of days later we receive an e-mail with the picture reminding me that, "Strangers are friends we just haven't met yet." I think Will Rogers said that.

Crow flies under sun.
His sweet small shadow cools me
And then he is gone.
Squirrel crosses road as
He carries a heavy load,
Acorns for dinner.

I get an early start today passing through Kellyville, Bristow, Depew, and across Little Polecat Creek. I cross back and forth over Interstate Rt. 44 many, many times. Lots of downhill slopes make an easy ride down and then I walk the bike uphill. Up and down, up and down all day, every day in the sun, the rain, and the clouds, "getting my kicks on Rt. 66." This morning's early start inspired several haikus:

Full white morning Moon,
Wants to stay and play with Sun
Just a little while.

I startled White Heron.
She flew and flew and I knew
She would reach the moon.

On early morning
Ride, my shadow's at my side.
We sing joyful songs.

Even billboards share poetry. Davenport said goodbye with a series of poetic signs.

Hope your visit
Was mighty fine.
Hope that sorehead
Didn't spoil your time
Cruising along,
My honey and me.

Rt. 66 is the place to be.

It's getting hotter every day but somehow I manage to bike 30-35 miles each day. A sign welcomes me to Warwick, Oklahoma, but I see only one building, Seaba Station. A rest station I need desperately. I hope it's air-conditioned. I am so hot and sweaty, I can smell myself. Jim is coming out of the place that looks like an old garage. "Sue, the owner, can't wait to meet you."

Sue's oasis is filled with antique dishes, furniture, toys, china, glass, jewelry, and all kinds of Rt. 66 souvenirs. I meet Sue, go pee, and then sit on a soft-cushioned stool, soaking in the cool air and the magical land of Americana that she's created here. We tell Sue about our pilgrimage, about Eric, and about some of the people we've met along the way.

"My devotional reading this morning said I was going to meet an angel today. I think you are that angel," Sue says.

"I'm not an angel but our last name is Angle and sometimes people do call us Angel."

"I knew it, you are an angel."

She tells us about the Oklahoma Rt. 66 Association and shares their website. We give her ours and take her picture for today's story on our website. I'm enchanted with her selection of jewelry. Although I just bought a Rt. 66 charm back in Chandler, I eye an unusual necklace, tiny glass beads holding a wire-wrapped stone.

"A woman collects the stones from a broken up stretch of Rt. 66 near Stanton, Illinois, and creates these treasures. Proceeds from the sale go to the preservation efforts for John's Modern Cabins, an abandoned tourist court near Newberg, Missouri."

I had to have one.

"Yes, you do," she says, "Pick one out as a gift from me."

I find one with blue beads and a round red stone. In return, I give her a copy of *Giving Sorrow Words*. I am rested and cooled, time to get back on the road. We hug and say goodbye.

> When Cloud kisses Sun,
> Soft breezes cool my body.
> I thank them both.

Down the road I pass a small white house with a front yard that looks like a desert oasis. The owner, a woman about my age, is watering her luxuriant flowers.

"How wonderful your garden looks out here in the middle of nowhere."

"Thank you. Come see my hidden pond with eight goldfish. For years and years I've been digging up rocks, planting and watering and digging the pond."

"I tried gardening and it's hard work."

"True, but what you're doing is really hard work."

I tell her why I'm walking and biking to Phoenix.

"Your son is looking down on you and keeping you safe," she concludes.

I know Eric is with me keeping me safe. Sometimes I feel he is speaking to me through other people. A local Cleveland columnist, Regina Brett, wrote about a friend of hers who completed suicide. She thought maybe instead of her friend taking her own life, she gave it back in a different form. That's how I feel about Eric sometimes. Because he chose to die, he gave me life by helping me become more compassionate, a more understanding person. I do understand human suffering more than I did before Eric's death.

Judy Collins said, "It's like you wake up … on a different planet. Your innocence is gone. You will never see the world in the same way." Joan Rivers told her, "You need to show up." Yes, we need to show up and do what we're supposed to do with our life. Right now I am supposed to walk and bike in Eric's memory and then write about it. Thank you, Eric, for giving me my purpose and for the gift of appreciating the beauty in this land as I slowly travel its roads.

Bright morning half moon
Leads my way then disappears
Returns for night-light.

Grasshoppers jump high.
They seem to fly as they hop
Reaching to the sky.

Bobwhite chirps. Bob-white
Sings. "Good morning, good morning,
Welcome to this day!"

We finally reach Oklahoma City, a city we'll remember. We celebrate our fifteenth anniversary at a rotating restaurant, Nikz at the Top, on the twentieth floor of an office building. As we toast our anniversary, we watch the sun set on the city below and thank God for bringing us safely this far on our journey.

Can't get out of town,
Busy streets, no sidewalks, flat
Tire, road ends. Help! Help!

We discover that Oklahoma City is not bike friendly. We drive out trying to find a safe and direct route out of the city. After many attempts, we succeed and put the tire on my bike only to discover a flat front tire, our first. The repairs bring out a few cuss words and loud remarks to each other. We are not looking forward to the day we have to change the back tire.

A bike path around Lake Overholser is in the right direction and we meet a fellow biker there, John, is riding an incumbent bike. He tells us about a bike path around the lake that connects with Rt. 66. It's a perfect day for a bike ride around a lake and I am feeling, what am I feeling? I am feeling joy. I remember an impromptu speech I gave in Toastmasters about joy:

Joy is a beautiful word. Joy reminds me of the song, "Joy to the world, all the boys and girls. Joy to the fishes in the deep blue sea, joy to you and me." Being joyful is important to me, especially during these past years. Joy used to mean making that last sale of the day, buying a new outfit, planning a dream vacation, or making lots of money. But my definition of joy has changed. Today joy is riding my bike on a sunny morning, listening to birds sing, and really seeing the reds, blues, yellow, pinks of summer flowers.

Joy is driving my convertible with the top down, the wind blowing my hair, the sun warming my face, and my husband sitting next to me, singing at the top of his lungs. Joy is stopping at the farmer's market to buy fruits and vegetables that were picked this morning. Joy is finding a perfect lamp at the last garage sale of the day.

Joy is "being" instead of "doing." It is being with my two-year-old grandson watching him chase butterflies. Joy is holding my three-month-old grandson watching him watching his world. Joy is the excitement of my daughter's becoming a mother again. I know she is going to have a girl just like her.

Joy is enjoying dinner with a special friend who gives me an unexpected gift, a porcelain heart that says, "Each day is a gift from God." It is hearing Maya Angelou speak in an auditorium of 3,000 people but feeling that she is talking just to me. Joy is being in the present moment but remembering and missing someone you love who is physically gone but with you always. Joy is being and appreciating every day. Yes, joy is a beautiful word.

Up ahead I see a pleasant scene, a man sitting in a folding chair, maybe fishing, a brown dog sitting at his side. As I ride by, I think, yes, it's even a perfect day to go fishing with your dog. As I ride by them, a man calls, "Iris!" The man is my husband. He's not fishing but talking on his cell phone to a client, his laptop computer perched on his lap. I stop to visit for a while and we laugh when I tell him I thought he was fishing. Joy, again.

I reach Rt. 66 and my smooth ride is over. The road to Yukon is heavily trafficked with no shoulder. Yukon is the home of Garth Brooks, which is well advertised on billboards around town. My next stop is El Reno but getting there is difficult. The road is stone and dirt all the way. I look behind me and realize I have company. A blonde dog, maybe a Labrador mix, follows me. He does not bark, just runs in front of me or follows me. I tell him to go home but he does not listen. After two miles I start to worry that he will not find his way home.

As I pass Moore's Towing, a man approaches to get a better look at the dog, thinking it is his. As he gets closer, he realizes that it is not, but he introduces himself as Terry.

"This dog has been following me for over two miles. I'm getting worried he won't find his way home."

The man's wife and daughter come out to see what the commotion is all about.

"How far are you riding today?" his wife asks.

I tell them about my journey. When I tell them I started from Chardon, Ohio, they stand stunned.

Terry says, "My wife Chris and I are from Ashtabula, Ohio, only thirty miles from Chardon." Terry gets a dish of water for the dog and holds him until I ride out of sight. I finish in the heat of the day after twenty-eight miles. Time to rest.

We head back to our hotel in Oklahoma City and decide it's time to get the bike checked. We find Al's Bike Shop and leave it overnight. Tomorrow will be a rest day for all three of us. Tonight we visit the Oklahoma National Memorial.

Chapter Seventeen

You'll Never Walk Alone

We sit under the
Survivor's Tree, we listen
We cry and we pray.

We do not know what to expect and are nervous about seeing it, but we must. As we approach the quiet, eerily beautiful site, the sun sets. We walk along the reflecting pool and stare at the Field of Empty Chairs, each of the 168 chairs honoring one person who was killed that day. As it grows dark, the glass in the base of the chairs illuminates and the field glows with a warm light. We are silent as we walk through the Gates of Time, the formal entry points to the memorial. The time 9:01 and 9:03 are set there forever. Neither Jim nor I speak as we walk to our car. We can no longer bear the pain.

We sleep in, a luxury, but we get restless by noon and decide to explore the city. First stop, Bricktown, the downtown entertainment district. A water taxi runs along the mile-long canal that winds through turn-of-the-century industrial buildings and warehouses that are now specialty shops and unique restaurants. We choose Chelino's Mexican Restaurant and sit outside, Biscuit quiet under our table for the entire meal until she sees three ducks swim by. She leaps away to jump into the water after them, but Jim grabs her collar just before she hits the water. She seems to enjoy the boat ride along the canal, though. At one end of Bricktown is the SBC Bricktown Ballpark, which is the home of the Red Hawks Triple A baseball team, the farm club of the Texas Rangers. Outside the park, statues of Mickey Mantle and

Johnny Bench greet baseball fans. At the other end of Bricktown, a fountain shoots water from holes in the ground. On this hot day, children run and jump through the water, laughing and squealing. Biscuit and I join the fun and run through the cool, refreshing water.

Back at the Oklahoma City Memorial, people walk silently along the reflection pool, considering the 168 empty chairs. We walk to the stone terrace where the Survivor Tree stands. In the explosion, a car landed in the tree and citizen's presumed the giant eighty-year-old American Elm would die. No, the tree chose to live and "now stands as a profound symbol of human resilience."

A crowd gathers as a park ranger appears and introduces himself as Ranger Alden. We sit on benches in the cool shade of that miracle tree and listen as he takes us back to that horrible day, April 19, 1995.

I remember the sun shining that day as I waited impatiently for spring. But spring did not come that day for 168 other people. A bomb exploded about 9:00 a.m. at the Murrah Federal Building where people had just begun another normal day. At the time no one knew why or who could have done such a destructive act--the number of people who had died or were missing was still unknown.

I remember praying on April 19 that they would all miraculously be found. What could I do but pray? I prayed that maybe I could take back a piece of my own world and change it. But to change the world, I must first change myself. How do I do that? What can I do? I have asked that question hundreds of times these past years. I learned that the work I must do first is to heal myself and then I can help others heal. My prayer that day was:

Dear God,

Please be with the families who lost loved ones in the Oklahoma City bombing. Help find those who are still in the rubble and we pray, are still alive. Give them strength and courage to get through this nightmare. Be with us all as we try to understand why things like this happen. Help us reach out to each other for comfort and support. Help us not to panic or to blame a group of people for the actions of a few fanatics. Comfort us all in these unsettling times. Help us to change ourselves so that we may change the world. Please help me believe that one day I will do something to change my world. Amen.

As my mind returns to the present, I hear stifled sobs and see tears on the faces of several people close to me as we listen. Jim and I hold hands. We talk to Alden for a few minutes and thank him for sharing that day with so much compassion and empathy. On a battered wall we read a handwritten message in big, black letters:

Team 5
4-19-95

We Search For the truth
We seek Justice.
The Courts Require it.
The Victims Cry for it.
God Demands it!

We walk along the fence that was erected to keep people off the site. Instead people began leaving memory artifacts on the fence and it became a part of the memorial. We walk along the chain fence and read the letters, notes, and poems, along with pictures, flowers, teddy bears, t-shirts, crosses, and the stories of the lives of the 168 people who died that day. And flags, flags flapping in the silence. I sensed that souls lingered on that memory-filled-fence. Again I pray:

Dear God,

Please still be with the loved ones of these people who left this earth too soon and too young. Even though it's been eight years, some are still grieving and need your comfort and healing. I pray that some have found meaning in their lives and experience joy, hope, and peace. Be with them on the anniversary of this tragedy and on all the days they need you. And thank you for sending me on this pilgrimage as my way of changing the world. I pray that I can complete this task. Amen.

Concert in the wind.
Sweet birds sing in harmony
Their own symphony.

Another hot day and a hilly road. I seem to go up, up and then down, up and down, then a stretch of straight four-lane road but with a wide berm, then down and down. I'm back on the almost deserted Rt.66 except for the people in the half dozen cars who wave and smile as we pass each other. The wind picks up and I am riding directly into it. I feel like the Wicked Witch of the East in the Wizard of Oz, peddling her bike in the tornado peddling, peddling, peddling but going nowhere.

I meet another live snake today, bigger than the first one I saw. It slithers away appearing to be more afraid of me than I am of it. Since entering Oklahoma, I prayed that I would not see a live snake or a tornado. So far: snakes-2, tornadoes-0. Thank You, God.

Between the wind and the heat, I am hot and tired and exhausted by noon. I can't remember the last time it rained and am so tired of the heat, the hills, the wind, this vast open land that keeps going and going. I can't get the image of the 168 empty chairs out of my mind. I think of all those families whose lives changed in one minute on one normal day. I think about how my life changed in one night. I must stay in the moment or be overcome.

I bike past yellow, gold, and green, green fields. Then I see purple cone plants, and Black-eyed Susans. Then fenced-in fields with cows and bulls grazing, paying no attention to this woman biking across their land.

Down the road I stop to admire a cross--tall, straight, and white. Pink, purple, red, white and yellow flowers wrap around it like a quilt keeping it warm. A tiny teddy bear sits in a comfy spot. In large letters on the horizontal piece is written MIKE.

Not too far down the road, I see another cross. The name and dates are carved into the brown wood, Jan, and the dates, 10-25-81 and 12-10-02. Yellow sunflowers, pink roses, a rainbow of zinnias, and a plastic bumblebee keep Jan company. Then another cross, no, not just one but three in a row. I can't read the names through my tears so I keep biking again staying in the moment.

All I see is death, death in front of me, death behind me, death beside me. I must stay in the moment, just keep biking. I follow the brown-paved-flat-endless road that touches a pale blue sky, nothing but road and sky. Is that what's ahead for me, nothing? I look down. Right in front of me is my shadow. The long-thin-dark-unrecognizable outline cannot be mine.

"What am I doing? What am I trying to prove? Why am I doing this? I'm not even half way on this phase and I have another third to go in the fall. I want to end this, now. Why am I putting myself through this physical torture when I've already experienced enough mental and emotional torture? Is it worth it? Is this crazy idea of mine making any difference to me, to my loved ones, to my world? I don't think so. It's a waste of time, money, energy and wearing out my already over 50-year-old body. I'm giving up, I'm quitting. Tonight I'll tell Jim I want to go home and get back to our lives. But how do I tell him I'm tired and want to go home?

I drag myself into the tub to soak while Jim reads our e-mails. I need time to find the words, to get up the nerve to tell him, "I quit, I want to go home." He is so quiet.

"Is anything wrong?" I ask.

"We received an e-mail from Sue at Seaba Station. I need to read it to you."

I get out of the tub, dry off, and put on my robe, thankful for the delay. "What does she say?"

"The subject line reads, 'You may have saved a life.'"

Dear Jim and Iris,

I sent an e-mail out to my Rt. 66 Association members telling them about our visit, your journey, and your website. I immediately received an e-mail from my friend, Mike. In his e-mail he wrote, "Thank you for the story, not only about Angle's walk across the county on Rt. 66 but her healing from her son's suicide. I've battled depression and considered suicide more than once. Recently I had a breakdown and knew I needed help. One night I was so depressed that I could not stop the tears from flowing. I even cried out, 'I don't want to die. This is God's work in action.' To seek help for my depression was the hardest decision I ever made but I had no choice if I want to live."

As Jim reads tears fill his eyes. We do not say a word but reach for each other and stand hugging, tightly and silently. I am shaking and need to sit down.

"I need to tell you something," I say. "I wanted to give up today, to go home. All day I thought about how I was going to tell you. I'm tired. I miss home and my friends. I feel like we're wasting our time, energy, and money. Sue's e-mail reminded me of the true reason of why I'm on this pilgrimage. Now I remember. God's work in action, again. Thank you, God, Sue, and Mike.

In her e-mail, Sue also shared this poem from *Giving Sorrow Words*.

Yes
It could happen any time, tornado,
earthquake, Armageddon. It could happen.
Or sunshine, love, salvation.

It could you know. That's why we wake
and look out--no guarantees
in this life.

But some bonuses, like morning,
like right now, like noon,
like evening.

--William Stafford

Another sunrise,
Wind blows stronger and harder.
I keep going.

We begin the day early enough to see our first sunrise on this phase, but even at this hour I know it's going to be another hot one. I am refreshed and excited knowing I made the decision to keep going, knowing we'll be in Amarillo soon and knowing we are reaching the end of the second phase. I am renewed in remembering why I'm doing this and in knowing I will complete this pilgrimage.

I bike through Weatherford, home of the Thomas P. Stafford Air and Space Museum, which is closed at this hour. I miss the road I'm supposed to take and end up biking a mile out of my way, meaning I have to bike a mile back. I am heading right into a strong south wind. I keep veering to the right but I'm on a service road with little traffic. Between the wind and the heat, I ride only 33 miles today. At this rate will I ever reach Amarillo?

In Elk City we visit the National Rt. 66 Museum. Pictures, murals, automobiles and vignettes depict the lives of those who lived, worked, and traveled the "Mother Road" in its beginning days. We meet Maxine, a volunteer who shares Rt. 66's history with anyone who will listen.

"Where's the best place to eat in town?"

"G's Garden serves the biggest, juiciest hamburgers in town."

"What do you like on yours?" We return after dinner with a well-done-plain-fat-juicy burger just the way she likes them.

> Always expect the
> Unexpected. That's what life
> is really about.

Our last town in Oklahoma is Erich. Spelled differently than my Eric but still the message is clear: "Keep going." The small town has a couple of businesses and a gas-station-grocery-store-coffee-shop-stop place. We both need a cup of coffee and a potty break. I meet Jim there before heading out of town. He's met Leon today, a local farmer who has lived here all his life:

"I remember the 'Mother Road' being built," Leon recalls. "Those were the days, so long ago. Now I have six children, thirteen grandchildren and nine great-grand-children. Life was good then. Life is good now, too. Godspeed on your journey."

I am hungry and buy peanut butter crackers from Tracy, working behind the counter. She heard us tell Leon about our journey, Tracy says, "My 16-year-old daughter died of an illness about a year and a half ago. I think of her every day."

"Grief is the hardest work we'll ever do, but we must do it if we want to heal."

She agrees with me. I give her a copy of Giving *Sorrow Words* and encourage her to write letters to her daughter. We hug. I even get a hug out of Leon before getting back on the road. We never know whom we will touch --or who will touch us.

I think about my friend and mentor Elizabeth who helped me to grow and to realize what a strong and determined woman I really was and continue to become. I worked as her assistant for almost three years and learned more from her than from any college course I took. Just recently I found an audio tape she made for me one month after Eric died. I didn't remember what she told me on this tape but today as I listen to it, I realize she gave me a gift of her wisdom to keep me going and help me heal:

"I want to formulate something to share with you to keep you smiling and loving and all those things you must do even though Eric is not here. You are a wise person, Iris, even though no one said anything to you to help you; you figured it out for yourself. In your struggle, you became wise by picking other people's brains to learn. You'll always cope because you became strong in your struggles.

"Don't blame Eric for leaving you. You will probably blame yourself, but you were not the only one who influenced him. You cannot take all the credit, others influenced him, too. Your role and how you played it is a result of the kind of person you are. You had his best interests at heart and you loved him.

"You feel a sense of waste of something good that has been thrown away. The loss of deep aching will never go away. I'd like you to read about Victor Frankl and logotherapy in his book, *Man's Search for Meaning*. He explains how pain about which you can do nothing nevertheless makes a part of you go on. He says, 'Turn suffering into achievement.'

"There is no reason to assume we can be successful at this immediately. Don't go around feeling good just to help others feel better, don't pretend. Take a long time. Have Jim around so you can cry on his shoulder.

"Use this time of introversion to rethink things, to get inspiration and learn to trust your God. Take advantage of this time of suffering to move on to some new level of awareness and feeling. Get together with friends and indulge yourself in talking, laughing, sharing, and healing."

I have achieved a new level of awareness, "turned my suffering into an achievement," and "indulged myself in talking, laughing, sharing, and healing" not with just my friends but also with people I meet along this path. Thank you, Elizabeth, Victor Frankl, and God.

> Roosters' crow, birds sing,
> Sun rises, moon disappears,
> A glorious day.

I reach the next town, Texola, Texas, if it could be called a town. Every building is boarded up tight, without sound or sight of civilization, a real western ghost town. Nothing looks like it has been used in years except the Baptist Church and I'm not even sure about that. I reach the border of Texas at 9:30 a.m., the 700-mile mark and my first forty-mile day. I sing, "The stars at night are big and bright deep in the heart of Texas!"

> Bluebonnets, gold sun-
> flowers, orange buttons, green earth,
> Garden of Eden.

> Wind blows from South,
> Leaning trees grow towards North,
> A Van Gogh painting.

We are staying at the Irish Inn in Shamrock, Texas, the only town with a hotel from the Oklahoma border to Amarillo, about one hundred miles. This means we backtrack several days. Everything in Shamrock is named either Shamrock or Irish, everything. Green billboards with Shamrocks welcome us into town. The two motels and two restaurants are Irish green. Green shamrocks decorate the town shops. The Irish Inn even has a piece of the Blarney Stone, which I touch for good luck. We read the Irish blessing in the motel lobby.

> May the road rise up to meet you.
> May the wind be always at your back.
> May the sunshine be warm upon your face,
> The rains fall soft upon your fields,
> And until we meet again may God
> Hold you in the palm of his hand.

In this flat, windy, and sparsely populated part of Texas, I bike six miles before seeing a car, through McLean home of the Devil's Rope Museum, closed today. This disappoints us as we learn the museum tells the history of barbed wire: its artifacts, its invention, and its impact on the development of the Old West. Murals on the old stone buildings depict scenes from early Rt. 66 and the first Phillips 66 service station built in Texas. One open gift shop entices me inside. I purchase a plain hematite bracelet because hematite aids healing.

The next town, Alanreed, is another ten miles down the road. Did I say town? The only thing in Alanreed is the gas-station-grocery-store-post-office-restaurant-beer-and-anything-else-you-need store. We chat with 80+ year-old Junior Davis, who had a seven-artery by-pass heart operation and failed kidneys. He's back to work, another survivor.

We are all survivors. Jim is a survivor of triple by-pass heart surgery in 1998. I remember that dark November day at University Hospital. The blue surgery cap sits askew on Jim's thin-gray hair. The anesthetic begins to make him drowsy but not before he tells one last joke. I kiss him goodbye and watch as they wheel him into surgery. We sit and wait and pray. His son Mark, and daughter-in-law, Mercedes; his daughter, Laura; his son Scott; my daughter, Laura; and our friend, Shannon, all wait and pray.

Other friends call or stop by to see how he is doing. Long hours later the doctor tells us, "He will be fine." Our friend Earl, a nurse practitioner, holds my hand as we walk into the recovery room. I want Earl to tell me Jim will be okay. Tubes protrude from every part of his body, his skin is ashen and his hair seems a little grayer. I see him smile and know he will be better than just okay.

Jim wrote this poem for me when he came home from the hospital.

The Healing Heart

She hovers over this mending heart. This heart long ago
unconditionally given to her. This heart not hard to love.

She does not mention the other heart breaking
day by day to see me suffer. I know this to be true.
Without the words these two hearts communicate.

She understands I am afraid but lets me have my humor.
I don't fool her with my jokes; she knows it's my attempt
    to say
"Honey, it's OK. This mending heart is still here and
    will return to you healed."

> Grazing goats greet me.
> Horses neigh hello, bulls glare,
> A great day to ride.

In this part of the country, Rt. 66 is mostly the service road for Interstate 40 and criss-crosses it for miles. In some places, Rt. 66 disappears, which means we drive on Interstate Route 40. Passing miles and miles of meadows and fields of magnificent wild- flowers, blue bonnets, and Indian paintbrush, and flat grasses where long-horn steers graze and lounge in the afternoon sun. The weather and wind cooperate and I bike another 40-mile day, two days in a row. I end in Groom, Texas. At dinner we ask our waitress what we should see while we're in Groom.

"They ain't nothin' in Groom."

She's right; there is nothing in Groom except two unusual artifacts. The "Cross of Our Lord Jesus Christ," standing 190 feet tall, is illuminated at night and is visible from twenty miles away. On the other side of the road sits the Leaning Water Tower, brought to Groom by Ralph Britten for his USA Truck Stop. He wanted a tourist attraction at his restaurant to give people a reason to stop. The truck stop disappeared, but the tower still stands tilted as another Rt. 66 oddity.

>My last day to ride,
>Heading toward Amarillo,
>And then home again.

I start biking at the tall cross early, sunny and cool, my last day on the bike for a while. The wind picks up just enough to let me know it's still with me. This land is so flat that there's not even one little hill to coast down to give my bottom a rest. And it really hurts. I get off and walk my bike just to rest it. I soak in the freshness of the air, the warm sun, and the silence. The only sound I hear are my tires hitting the ground as they go round and round. I add a few verses to my chant.

Wild flowers growing,
Heavenly breezes blowing
For all my friends and family,
And those we just met.

I Thank you. I Thank you.
Namaste, I Thank you.

I'm biking and chanting and being in the moment, when I see something sitting in the middle of the road. Is it a dead animal? No it moves slightly. Is it a live animal? I approach it slowly, cautiously. Then I see Jim sitting cross-legged in the middle of the road. "What are you doing?" I shout.

"I'm waiting for you like I've been doing this past month."

"In the middle of the road?"

"I didn't want to miss you."

"Well I couldn't miss you!" We laugh and hug and I continue on.

Jim has always waited for me. He waited for me to say yes to his fifth marriage proposal. He patiently helped me finish my education. He waits for me to put on my "jewels" before going out. He waited for me to come out of my deep depression. He waited for me as I cried on his shoulder night after night. He waited for me to be healthy and whole again.

He waited for me to decide when to be intimate again. The first time we made love after Eric died, I cried and cried afterward because I felt alive again. With Jim's help and love, I knew I was going to live. And now he waits for me in the middle of the deserted road.

I reach Amarillo at the thirty-mile mark of my day. I ride past the airport and what I think was at one time the Air Force base, deserted long ago. Rt. 66 converges with Rt. 60, heavily trafficked at this hour and without a shoulder. Together Jim and I decide that this is the end of the trail for this second phase of my journey. We haul the bike into the car and drive a short distance to the Amarillo city limit sign to take a picture. We are tired and it's time to go home.

Killdeer run with me
Then fly up and run on road.
Once more I can fly.

July 1, 2003

I came to visit you today.
It was so dark, I could not stay.
The wind hurt, the ground hard.
Standing there, I cried out loud.
Dry leaves cover your black stone.
And shivering, I'm alone.
Sometimes, I want to be with you,
But I still have work to do.

Dear Eric,

What a perfect way to begin a new journal, a letter to you while sitting at your grave. I know you're not here but it comforts me to see your name written in the black stone. The inscription, "He gave us love and laughter," reminds me that you really did live, and live fully.

I've never been to your grave at this time of day. The setting sun sneaks behind the giant maple that sits too far from your grave to give you shade from the hot summer sun. But Gabe's dad is nearby and your policeman friend keeps you company. I pulled the weeds and cut back dried irises from May. You need some new decorations.

We made it home yesterday from the second phase of our journey. I felt your presence every day on the road. Thank you for keeping me safe, especially when I had that close call. Did you ever think that your mom could have biked and walked such a long distance? I could not have done it without God, Jim, you, our friends, and the people we met along the way. One more phase to go and then this journey will end. I wonder what my next one will be? Perhaps writing a book about this one.

I can't believe I walked and biked 789 miles in 26 days. The idea is still sinking into my brain. Just like it took several years for my brain to accept the fact that you chose to die. You knew I was a survivor but did you have any idea that I would be doing all the things I've done to honor our love? I sure didn't.

I did something today I haven't done in a long time, too long. I drove to Mentor Headlands Beach. I lay on the hot sand and fell asleep. I dreamed of you and me racing our bikes down Bass Lake Road, laughing and flying. I woke up smiling and then a memory came to me:

One summer afternoon when you were two or three years old, we came to this beach, you loved the water and played all afternoon running between the water and the sand, and then you disappeared. Our friends walked the beach, the parking lot, and the playground. As the minutes passed without a sign of you, I imagined you floating on the water. I was scared until I heard your dad shout, "He's here, I found him." I held you so tight that you cried.

And now I hold my memories.

It's strange to be here at this time of night. Almost the entire back of the cemetery is shaded by the few giant maple trees. Birds sing and a dog barks in the distance but it's mostly silent. I've grown accustomed to the silence these past ten years, especially here. I've visited you in drizzling rain, three feet of snow, black, gray, white clouds, hot, hot sun, but never at sunset. I like it. I'm comfortable and at peace. Thank you, God. And thank you, Eric.

I have to go but I promise to come back soon to spend time thinking and writing to you. I'll bring you some new decorations. Love, Mom

August 5, 2003

On my 55th birthday I'm sitting on the patio of the con-do we've been renting for a month in Pinehurst, North

Carolina. The sun peeks through an overcast sky. I finished reading *The Art of Pilgrimage, The Seeker's Guide to Making Travel Sacred,* by Phil Cousineau. We learn from every pilgrimage, the author writes. What have I learned from these two phases of my pilgrimage?

1. I am able to ride my bike for forty miles in one day.
2. I can ride or walk every day for at least 26 days.
3. I can ride/walk in rain, heat, hills, unpaved roads, city, country roads, city sidewalks, dirt paths, and I can pee wherever I need to.
4. Solitude is healing.
5. I cannot make my journey alone.
6. I meet all kinds of people: hurting, grieving, happy, content, and life-loving. They come in various shapes and sizes; colors of skin, hair, and eyes; and tone of voice, some warm and some cold.
7. Our country's landscape is as diverse as its people.
8. If I can walk and bike every day, I can write and heal every day.
9. I can make more pilgrimages.
10. I can share my story and the stories of those I meet. Our stories can heal the world.

What will I learn at the end of my pilgrimage?

Oct. 15, 2003

Dear Eric,

I came to clean your grave. I brought you a pumpkin with a funny face, a new chime, and a Frankenstein doll. I can't stay long but I'll visit you after the end of our journey which will be after Thanksgiving. We're leaving next week for the last phase and plan to be in Phoenix on your birthday. I know you'll be with me as I bike through the strange, different and difficult desert-land. The desert reminds me of your final decision, of the pain and loneliness you felt and the reality that you are dead.

I cannot think of that now.

Today the sun is shining but it's cool and breezy. I wonder what it will be like in New Mexico--hot, cold, flat, or mountainous. I wonder who I'll meet and what the people are like. I'm getting excited but I'm also nervous about this final phase. You are with me always. Love, Mom.

Chapter Eighteen

Let It Be

October 29, 2003: The Third Phase Begins

> Beginning again,
> Past - Future thoughts guide me to
> The Present moment.

I'm sitting in a doctor's office listening to the Beatles sing, "Let It Be," realizing it is also my prayer which is what I am now saying. Dear God, please be with Jim as he goes through this procedure. Give him strength, comfort, healing, and love. Amen.

Jim is having a prostate biopsy. I'm trying to stay in the now, in my body. I want to be the portal between my body, my mind, my soul, and God as I sit here waiting. Jim scheduled a check-up last week and tests revealed a high PSA count. The doctor wanted to do a biopsy before we left. We had to wait a week for this appointment, a week at home with no plans, nothing to do but worry, think, and pray.

I want to be in the Now. I want that feeling I experienced on the road: praying, exercising, admiring the beauty of the world, visiting with people, my body exhausted at night, stretching and soaking in the tub, reuniting with Jim at the end of the day sharing our experiences, being in the moment. How can I keep that feeling?

We will not have the biopsy results for another week. The doctor said if Jim was feeling good tomorrow, we could leave the day after. We can worry on the road just as easily as we can worry at home. We ask each other, "How are you doing?" We both answer, "Okay." But are we?

We do not talk about the biopsy but it consumes our thoughts. If Jim has cancer, we will deal with it just as we dealt with Eric's death. We'll cry and pray and go on living. But the question would be "how well?" We did get through his triple-heart- bypass in 1998, we will get through this, too.

As we drive to Amarillo, I listen to a CD, *The Power of Now,* by Eckhart Tolle. He says now, this present moment, is all we have but we, no, I tend to live in the past. I think about Eric and how much I miss him. I still ask the question; how could he leave this earth, how could he leave me? Sometimes I think about what life would have been like had Eric not killed himself. Would he be married and have children? What would he be doing now? What would I be doing now? Certainly not biking and walking across the country.

If I'm not thinking about the past, the future looms in my mind. I worry about Laura and her family. I worry about Jim's health, especially now. I worry about being able to finish this journey. Jim's dad is ninety-four, and could die any day. And then there's the condition of the world and this war in Iraq. Always there's something to worry about and keep me from being in the present moment. Now, just drive.

Today is November 1, All Saints' Day. We've been on the road since 8:00 a.m. and now are in Oklahoma with over a hundred miles before we reach Amarillo, Texas. The dark, gloomy day reminds me of November in Ohio. It's sprinkling lightly. I hope the weather clears by tomorrow. I can't believe I'll be starting the last leg of my journey in the morning.

Jim slept and I drove from Strand to Clinton, Oklahoma, staring at the road I bicycled in June. We pass familiar names of the places we ate and stayed and rested. As we drove through Erich, Oklahoma, I thought about Tracy and Leon. I remember this part of the ride being warm and sunny with fields of wildflowers along the road.

I think about the All Saints' Day Helen and I celebrated in 1994, a year after Eric died. In Spanish All Saints' Day is called El Dia de Los Muertos, the Day of the Dead. On this day families gather together at their loved ones' graves to celebrate, honor, and remember their loved ones by sharing their favorite meal.

On that dark, gloomy November day, Helen and I took a picnic lunch to Eric's grave. As we ate cheese and crackers and drank a glass of wine, I told her about Eric, whom she never got to meet. I told her about the day he died and how I felt I had died with him. We felt his presence among us. We wrote a poem so we would remember the day.

Cool day, fallen leaves scatter on your grave.
Bells ring. Where are you, Eric?
Silly question, we know you are here,
Having wine with us, wishing it was beer.
No smoking, though, it's bad for your health.
Rain begins to fall as we leave you here
Physically, but we keep you in our hearts.
We miss you and we are healing.

Time to get back to NOW.

In Texas again,
Ready to ride through sun, wind
And rain. Soon the end.

I begin at the exact spot where I ended in June, the outskirts of Amarillo where Rt. 66 meets Rt. 60. It's Sunday, traffic is as light as the rain. I ride and think and pray soaking in this flat, hot, and windy state. Will it be hot, windy, and flat all the way across? Thank goodness I'm only biking across the panhandle and not the middle of the state. I'd never reach the end.

Time for a rest. I am in the shopping district of the city and spot a Barnes and Noble. Of course I have to go in, browse, and pee. I find three gems; a book on writing poetry for children, Judith Viorst's *If I Were in Charge of the World,* and a children's storybook called, *The Armadillo from Amarillo.* I still haven't seen a live egg-shaped armadillo, just dead flat ones.

I continue riding through the city and on the other side I come to Cadillac Ranch where Jim is waiting. We stopped here last June. An eccentric millionaire, Stanley Marsh, III planted ten vintage Cadillacs nose-down in a wheat field west of Amarillo. Each car represents the style change of the car's tail fins from 1949 to 1963. Last June all ten Cadillacs were painted black in memory of Doug Michaels, one of the project's artist-creators.

They are no longer black but are now--spray painted in rainbow colors by people who leave messages. I have no spray paint but I write my message in red ink. I draw a heart and inside I write, "Biking from Ohio to Phoenix, Iris, Jim and Biscuit, 11/2/03." We take a picture. I am bundled in my green jacket over my black jacket, two pairs of pants, my helmet, and biker's gloves—and still wondering what I am doing.

> My long tall shadow
> Slowly creeps toward me keeping
> Me sweet company.

After a short rest I get back on my bike. The sun comes out and I strip off both jackets and one pair of pants. I reach a little burg called Bushland, the end of my first day back on the trail.

I am in the present moment, feeling the warm sun on my back, seeing the wind swirl the leaves in a spiral taking them for a ride, then letting them fly to amuse me. I breathe in this present moment.

Every day is the same. Every day is different. I bike, I walk, I rest, and I do it again the next day, except today. Shortly after starting out, I have a flat tire. We change it at the Shell station where we ended yesterday. I tell the owner, "This service station is the cleanest one I have been in and I've been in more than I can remember." With a big grin, he says, "Thank you."

It's sunny but windy and getting windier as I struggle across the Texas panhandle. The wind wears me out and my bottom hurts. In Vega, a short distance down the road, we put the bike in the car and I walk with Biscuit. She keeps stopping and looking back. We walk like this until I can no longer stand it. She must think we left Jim behind. I call him, "Please come pick up your dog. She thinks we left you."

Alone again, I see a dead coyote along the side of the road. Far back, in phase one I created a ritual of blessing the soul of dead animals whenever I pass one. I bless this one and continue on.

I learned about ritual at the 1995 *Common Boundary* conference, called "Inner-Outer Ecology." In a workshop with Matthew Fox, an Episcopal priest, I learned the Steps to Ritual:

Leave the ordinary: I haven't experienced the ordinary in days, weeks, years.

Enter sacred space. Sacrifice, call on energies: I've called on God's energy since I began this healing journey and will continue to call on his/her energy. I witness this sacred space as I walk and bike. Connecting with the earth, saying my daily prayers, sharing my story and hearing other's stories, just being in the moment are my ways of entering a sacred space.

Instruction: I listen to God and follow his instructions.

The Test: Stand in the middle of tension and hope and pray for our planet-- Is this why I bless the dead animals I see along the road?

Celebration for having passed the test: I'm still taking the test.

Thanksgiving-energy and spiritual angels: my thanksgiving chant and prayers.

Return to the ordinary: will that be possible?

At the same conference I learned from another speaker, Andrea Olsen, a professor and author that we must learn to connect our own body with the earth by engaging in life. We do this by: being willing to recreate as we create; being comfortable with not knowing; and understanding that we are a part of everything we see, that touch underlies vision, and that the more open we are to our perception, the more able we are to understand.

I wrote my journal, I wanted to walk someplace I've never walked before and here I am walking across the country connecting to the earth and engaging in life like I never imagined and comfortable not knowing what lies ahead or what the day may bring. I believe we are a part of everything. Is that why I say a prayer for the dead animals? Will I understand more about where I fit into this world with every step I take? And in this silence will I hear the answer?

"The necessary thing is, after all, but this: solitude, great inner solitude. Going into oneself and for hours meeting no one-- this one must be able to attain."

Letters to a Poet,
Rainer Maria Rilke

In my solitude I remember this letter to Eric:

Journal Entry
November 3, 1993

Dear Eric,

I walked to Tinker's Creek today, a walking trail through woods and around seven ponds. I haven't been there in a long time but it's warm and sunny for early November. I want to walk somewhere I've never walked before, somewhere far away. I'll think about that, walking somewhere far, far away. As I walked today, I also thought about some of the books I've been reading. I don't remember where I read this but I want to share it with you:

November is your birthday month. It's also the month of finishing our business, of squaring the inner and outer accounts that require our energy. One way we come to completion is through grieving for those who have died this past year and celebrating the things we shared and learned together. I think that's what I'm trying to do in these letters to you.

Meditations and rituals of grieving and completion include forgiveness, that attitude of mind that sets us free when we are able to claim our wisdom and move on. In forgiving ourselves and others, we pave the way for atonement, At-One-Ment between all people and our creator. November completions clear the way for the birth of Inner Light in December.

November is a month sacred to the Archangel Raphael, the Healer. To heal, to be whole is to reconcile our accounts so that all is in balance. Forgiveness is a way to Reconciliation, a path made easier because it is lighted and maintained by the angels of grace.

"We may reap unforgiving thoughts from our own children-- because we have sowed unforgiving thoughts toward our own parents." That statement hit me; no-- slapped me, in the face. Did my unforgiving thoughts and words toward my mother, step-father, and father model your own unforgiving feelings toward me—and worse—toward yourself perhaps leading to your suicide? Did you die to help me understand how to work on my unforgiving thoughts, to learn forgiveness? What a painful way to learn a lesson and what a sacrifice you had to make. Was this your life purpose?

If so, then I must learn my lesson, I must heal, find my life purpose and live it. What do I do, Eric, with this new knowledge? I also learned that we all are doing the best we can, given our own circumstances and our own individual soul unfolding, and that includes my mom, step-father, you, and me.

Forgiveness is based on understanding of others; if we understand those who wronged us, we can forgive them. Forgiveness is a matter of changing our mind. Of forgiving the debt. Affirming the abundance. Today at Tinker's Creek, I asked the Archangel Raphael to help me heal in this month of forgiveness and in this month of your birth.

I forgive myself. I forgive you, Eric. I forgive. Thank you, God, for giving me this understanding.

Laura called last night upset. She was looking for a birthday card for your Uncle Ed, his birth month, too. Uncle cards are right next to brother cards. When she saw all the brother cards, she began to cry because she couldn't remember the last time she sent you a card. I couldn't remember what we did on your birthday last year and I started to cry with her.

I cried when you were born.
I cried when you died.
I cried today. I'll cry tomorrow.
When will I stop crying?

When will I have enough understanding and forgiveness to stop crying for us both? Eric, I love you and miss you, Mom

After lunch I get on my bike only to discover another flat tire, this time the back one. With little difficulty Jim tackles the gears and unknown parts, and changes the tire with not one swear word. I am shocked. We drive to a gas station to put air in the tire. We end up driving to four stations; one had no air pump, two had no working pumps, finally success. We pump air in the tire but it blows a defective inner tube. Back to the motel to get another tube and change it. Experts now, we change it quickly.

I get back on the road. The wind blows harder now and dust tears my eyes. After only two miles, I give up for the day. Just for the day. I know I must keep going and I write this poem.

> In the panhandle of Texas
> While fighting the wind,
> I wondered if I would reach the end.
> I looked back to see
> How far I'd come,
> Then I hear his voice say,
> "Keep going. You can do it, Mom."

Texas may be flat and windy but its sunrises are poetry and paradise. I'm already on my bike when the sun greets me good morning in all her glory. I feel she welcomes me to this new, strange territory. It is cold and the wind blows hard. Will it be like this all day?

I bike four miles and the road ends, just disappears. We drive fifteen, twenty miles on the interstate before we find it again, now in New Mexico, Land of Enchantment. Back on the bike for a few more miles before the road disappears again. We discover the road will disappear and reappear all the way through New Mexico.

When I am biking, the wind is so fierce I feel like I'm peddling, peddling, and going nowhere. Out of curiosity I turn around and bike in the opposite direction. With the wind at my back pushing me, I relax and wish I could ride like this all the way to Phoenix. It is easier to go back to the past, we don't have to live it again just look at it and remember or forget. However, it does not take us where we want to go, where we need to go.

I want to end this journey as fiercely as I wanted to end the nightmare of Eric's death. I am so tired, then I hear Eric's words, "Keep going, turn back west, you can do it, Mom." I look down at the bracelet that Zach gave me when I walked the marathon for him. He didn't give up and now he's a healthy ten-year-old. I think of my friend Frieda who struggles with cancer, yet doesn't give up.

I turn around and head west towards the finish line, towards the future.

Chapter Nineteen

Only Love

Morning fireworks burst,
Blue-red-orange-yellow-gold sun
Awakening to greet me.

Just outside Tucumcari, New Mexico, I give my bottom a rest and walk for a while. Coming into town, I notice a flattop mountain in the distance and wonder about its name. In this charming Western town, I first stop at a bookstore, of course. I find a book by Elie Wiesel and a poetry book about the people and places along Rt. 66. Next stop is a gift shop called the Teepee, shaped like a real teepee. I buy postcards and a Rt. 66, 2004 calendar.

After dinner we go into Gifts Unique & Boutique owned and operated by Molly. I did not bring a winter jacket and it's colder here than I had anticipated. Jim picks out a black fleece jacket with a wolf on the front and back. At first I do not like it, but when I put it on, it's warm and cozy like an old blanket that never wears out.

I spot a postcard on the counter picturing the flat-top mountain I saw this morning. The back explains: "Tucumcari Mountain is a unique topographic butte southeast of the city with an elevation of 4,956 feet. The city is named for the mountain, which has an old Indian legend.

"Apache Chief Wautonomah lived on the mountain with his tribe. He lived a long life but was nearing death and had no sons who could take his place as chief, only a daughter, Princess Kari. His two finest braves, Tonopah and Tocum, rivals and sworn Enemies, both wanted Princess Kari. Secretly her heart belonged to her true love, Prince

Tocum. The chief arranged a knife battle to the death between the two rivals--the winner would be the new chief and husband of Princess Kari. The braves battled until Tonopah killed Tocum. Kari, overcome with grief, grabbed a knife and killed Tonopah and then herself. The chief, grief stricken, plunged the knife into his own heart and cried out in agony. "Tocum-Kari!" Death again.

> Now my shadow friend
> Leaves me all alone to ride
> Fierce Wind fighting me.

This is new territory for us, land Jim and I have seen only on TV western movies. Mornings are sunny and cool, so I dress accordingly: bike pants over long tights, t-shirt, Jim's sweatshirt because I forgot mine and my lime green bicycle jacket with the orange reflecting vest. By noon it's so hot I'm down to my t-shirt and bike pants. This barren land has no gas stations for miles. No trees to hide behind to pee, Jim holds a blanket up by the car to give me privacy. So few cars drive by, this is probably not necessary.

This is cattle country: bulls, steers, horses, and an animal that looks like a cross between a goat and a deer. Jim did see a roadrunner cross the road, but still no live armadillos. The tiny town of Newkirk looks deserted until I see a house with clothes drying on the line. Two dogs bark and chase me. I tell them sternly to go home.

To my right Interstate Rt. 40 sits so close I can see and hear the cars and trucks flying by. To my left, mile-long trains zoom by on rattling tracks. Ahead of me are wide-open, clear, blue sky and the red rock mesas. Finally we happen upon a country store where we stock up on goodies for lunch, no restaurants out here. We reach for a tuna sandwich in the cooler when a truck driver suggests we look at the expiration date before we buy it. Maybe crackers with peanut butter and V-8 juice would satisfy our appetites. Tomorrow we'll pack our lunch.

Back on the road with the sun shining, the temperature comfortable, the land flat and a blasting wind. We use the walkie-talkies because I forgot to charge my phone battery. Not much chance of getting lost out here with only two roads, Rt. 40 and its service road that I'm biking. I keep heading west.

I bike into and through Santa Rosa, New Mexico, "City of Natural Lakes," in five minutes, up a gradual hill and then fly down. We stop for a late breakfast-early lunch at a Rt. 66 diner. Pictures of James Dean and Marilyn Monroe cover the walls. The décor, early Coca-Cola with 1950's furniture, permits time to stand still in this little bit of heaven.

We see two places we want to explore at the end of the day. Jim's choice is the Rt. 66 Auto Museum, "dedicated to the preservation and exhibition of Route 66-era automobiles and other related objects of Car Culture interest--'Anything to do with wheels!'" James "Bozo" and Anna Cordova share their collection of classic Rt. 66 custom cars and memorabilia in an enjoyable and entertaining atmosphere "just to have some fun." The museum holds over thirty mint-condition cars from the 50's and 60's along with historic pictures and Rt. 66 items for sale. Jim takes my picture standing between James Dean and Marilyn Monroe posters.

My choice is the Blue Hole. When I saw the sign, memories surfaced. Could there be another Blue Hole? I grew up in Castalia, Ohio, much smaller than Santa Rosa but home of "THE Blue Hole"--its only claim to fame. The full depth is unknown but the visible depth is 50-60 feet down, fed by an underground river with a year-round temperature of forty-eight degrees. At least once a week I walked to the Blue Hole to look down to try to find the carriage that is said to have fallen into it a hundred years ago. I never did see it. But carriage or no carriage, Castalia's Blue Hole always mesmerized me with its glowing azure light coming from a great distance below the surface of the clear water—a true mystery that left summer tourist crowds in deep silent awe of nature. And of what strangeness was possible right there in homey Ohio countryside.

Now we follow the signs leading us to this Blue Hole. When I see the clear water, I know this place. We walk around the fence and look down into the small round pond that looks like a giant well. A sign on the fence explains that it's approximately eighty-one feet down. Divers from all over the world gather here to hone their diving skills. We are the only people here and it is eerily quiet as we gaze at our reflections in Santa Rosa's Blue Hole.

As we drive away, Jim's phone rings. His doctor is calling with the biopsy report. We hold our breaths. "Negative, no cancer." And we say a prayer of thanksgiving.

Today we drive sixty miles as no service road exists. At this rate we'll be in Phoenix sooner than we planned. At Moriarty I bike the rest of the day until I have to find a place to pee, no service stations for the last thirty miles. I do see a sheet metal factory which looks new, and clean, posting a sign, "Public Welcome." This forward- thinking company acknowledges that service stations are rare in this part of the country! When I come out of the restroom, Jim has put my bike in the car because its 4:30 and the sun sets around 5:00 this time of year, too dark to bike.

Before we left, I sent a press release to *The Arizona Republic*, the Phoenix daily telling them about my journey. Angela, a reporter, contacted Laura for an interview. Now Laura calls after the interview upset and crying. "Oh, mom, a reporter named Angela asked me questions about Eric's mental state and if he left a note. I showed her a copy of his note. Then later, I thought maybe I shouldn't have. I can't stop crying."

"It's alright, honey. You did the right thing sharing your feelings. And it's okay that you showed her his note."

"She wants to talk to you before you reach Phoenix. I gave her your cell number," Laura added. "I can't wait to see you in a couple of weeks. I love you"

"Me, too."

A little while later Angela calls and interviews me on the phone as we drive into Albuquerque.

"I interviewed your daughter and wanted to ask you a few questions about what you are doing," Angela explained.

"Yes, I talked to her. She was surprised to have a reporter come to her home. But thank you for taking an interest and writing about my journey."

"I have read your website so I don't have many questions about your journey. But tell me about Eric. Did you have any idea he would take his own life?"

"No, it was a complete shock to me and to everyone he knew."

"Your website states that you write letters to him in your journal. What kinds of things do you write to him?"

"I miss him. I wish he were still alive. I didn't understand why he did it. Sometimes I write about anger, grief, and how depressed I am without him."

"Are you going to have any kind of ceremony at the end?"

"I think so I'm but not sure what it will look like yet."

"How do you think you will feel when you finish your journey?"

"I don't know yet. I'll be tired and excited about seeing my daughter and grand-children. I know Eric was with me every step, every mile, and every day of this trip."

"I'd like to interview you in person before you get to Phoenix. Can you call me when you get about fifty miles outside of Phoenix? When do you think that will be?"

"At the rate we're traveling, we should be in Phoenix two days earlier than we planned, either Wednesday or Thursday, instead of Friday which is Eric's birthday.

We told her we'd be coming through Globe and Superior and would call her when we got to those towns.

"We'll see you in a couple of weeks, Angela. And thank you for helping us raise public awareness of suicide prevention."

This conversation reminds me of a letter I wrote to Eric.

August 30, 1995

Dear Eric,

I see your smiling face and sometimes your not so smiling face. I still ask why. I feel I am moving towards coming to terms with your being gone and the choice you made. I will always love you and I know you felt that you were doing the right thing for you. I'm on a plane flying to Phoenix to visit Laura and Alec. The sky is so blue and the ground a patchwork quilt. I'm going back to where you died. I am always sad when I think about you out there in the desert alone. What were your last days like? Your last hours? Minutes? What were you thinking? I'll never know, maybe when I see you one sweet day. Will you be able to give me an answer? Why did you drive out into the desert? Why and how did you choose this place? To be alone in your loneliness? I didn't know you were so lonely, afraid, mixed-up, depressed, and angry? All those emotions strong enough, powerful enough for you to make that final decision. Was it a mistake? Did you want to take it back after you pulled the trigger? Were you in physical pain after the shot? I never thought or asked that question. It's too painful for me to think about. I pray an angel came to take you into the light. I pray that you are at peace. I love you and miss you. Love, Mom

"In the desert, there is all and there is nothing. God is there and man is not."

Balzac

207

The next day we drive back to Edgewood, "Where the Mountains meet the Plains on Historic Rt. 66" and where we ended yesterday. Early and bitter cold, we stop at a store to buy gloves and a headband to keep my ears and hands warm. The ride into Albuquerque is all downhill, delightful. I ride through Tijeras Canyon separating the Sandia and the Manzano Mountains, popular with bikers. I see other bikers on the road and we nod hellos. I focus on the houses hanging over the cliffs, not paying attention, when a biker zooms past me as if I'm standing still.

I discover Albuquerque is bike friendly. A bike path winds through the city running parallel to Interstate Rt. 40. A chain-link fence and sometimes a cement wall separates the highway from the path. Jim keeps calling me to keep track of where I am. He gets nervous when he doesn't know my exact location. The path ends by a golf course, which I ride through until I come into a residential section. We settle on a location to meet and call it a day.

I have not written a haiku for a couple of days, but I don't know why. Talking to the reporter and knowing we'll be in Phoenix in two weeks makes this phase so different from the others. This foreign landscape and knowing I'm close to the end of my journey both excites and frightens me. How am I going to feel when I finish? I don't want to think about it now.

I want to think about this passage on beauty from Ralph Waldo Emerson:

"Never lose an opportunity of seeing anything that is beautiful, for beauty is God's handwriting--a sacrament. Welcome it in every fair face, in every fair sky, in every fair flower and thank God for it is a cup of blessing."

How do I describe this beauty, this blessing? Along the miles between Santa Rosa and Albuquerque I see only an unending road, twisting and turning and then straight into the horizon, without trees or bushes, just dry brown ground. Then I spot a bare tree keeping company with a roofless building that displays a faint-painted "cold beer" sign, nothing else. Another few miles till I pass a cemetery with old, leaning stones protected by a wire fence holding a giant white cross. Then, a "dead end' sign forces us to drive a few miles.

Back on Historic Rt. 66, I pass a relic of the old Mother Road, a rusty gas pump in front of a car so old and rusted that I do not recognize the model. Painted on the brown door is, "Busted on 66." The car sits next to a falling-down building that posts "Danger, No Trespassing." More crosses on the side of the road, then more nothing for miles and miles.

I think back to the beginning of my grief journey. I could see no road, could see no tomorrow, and could see nothing but a brown box, a black stone, and white snow. I felt old like that cemetery and the only thing holding me up was writing letters to Eric. I pretended he was on a trip and if I kept writing the letters he would read them when he got home. But then I remembered, he was dead. Then I would have a memory or a dream which kept me going for a few days. I saw no beauty in my life, just depression, sadness, loneliness, anger, guilt, regret, nothingness. And definitely no cup of blessing--until now. Now I thank God for the opportunity of seeing the beauty of this land and entering into this sacrament.

It takes us an entire day to get out of Albuquerque. First we meet our friends, Sue and Reed, for coffee at the Starbucks in Old Towne where I will start biking. They are driving to their second home in Scottsdale, Arizona. Before we meet them we stop to put air in the bike tires. As we drive to Starbucks, we hear a loud pop and Biscuit jumps into my lap. The Slime Tube inner tube on my bike has blown. Green, gunk-glob flows over the backseat onto our belongings. We clean it up and change tires with Reed laughing and Sue taking pictures. We say good-bye but will see them in Phoenix at the end of our trip.

I finally get on the road and bike down Rt. 66, across the Rio Grande and out of the city. A couple of miles out of town, I have another flat tire. We change it and I get on the road again. We have learned about goat heads, tiny thistles with sharp, spiky thorns. Jim reminds me to stay away from them. I see the "Leaving Albuquerque" sign and want to take a picture of my bike leaning against it. Carefully I pick up my bike, set it next to the pole, take a quick picture, pick it up and place it back on the road. To my horror, both tires are covered with goat heads. I pick them off and get back on the road.

Jim calls to say he accidentally got onto Interstate Rt. 40 and had to go up to the next exit to turn around. I have another flat tire. I walk my bike for a couple of minutes when a woman stops.

"Do you need help? Would you like a ride to the gas station up ahead?" She drives me and my bike in her SUV up to the gas station at the exit where Jim will get off of Rt. 40. Cindy, a long-distance bike rider, rode the Lake Tahoe 100-mile ride for the Leukemia and Lymphoma Society. Jim arrives and I introduce him to Cindy. He's not too happy about my getting in the car with a stranger. But she's not a stranger anymore. We say good-bye and I give her a copy of *Giving Sorrow Words*.

We change my tire and I get on the road again. I bike merrily along wondering how far I will get this time. A group of twenty bicycle riders flies past me as I slowly bike out of the city. As they disappear, another tire blows, my last inner tube.

Time to quit for the day, nine miles, my shortest distance in the longest time. I'm tired. Jim is too. We drive to a Wal-Mart but no inner tubes. We ask for directions to a bike shop where we leave the bike overnight for a check-up. The boy who works there tells us, "Because we have these goat

heads, bikers in this part of the country use extra thick inner tubes. Would you like me to put those on your bike?"
"Yes, yes," we both shout. No more flat tires!

> Sleeping dog, rays of
> sun shining down on her face.
> All is well in our world
>
> Friendly dogs follow
> me as I ride rolling hills.
> All is well with my world.

The terrain changes from flat to gently rolling hills and in the distance I begin to see red flat-top mountains. I ride across the Laguna Indian Reservation, which is dry, barren, and suitable only for grazing. Small pueblos dot the landscape. In the distance, I see a long, flat gray building and read the neon flashing sign, Dancing Eagle Casino, civilization but barely. The strong wind tires me, and soon I pass a gas station that looks like its last customer died ten years ago.

Two pit bulls, one brown and the other black, follow me about four miles. I stop a highway worker and ask, "What should I do about these dogs?" He assures me that they will get tired and go home. They don't. They waddle in the middle of the road and I picture a car flattening them. The brown one is friendly and he lets me see the license around his neck, Tiger plus his phone number. Jim tries to call the owner but no one answers.

They follow me until I see a truck with "Dog Warden" sign on its door. He stops and asks if these are my dogs. I call Jim to tell him what's happening. He drives up as an old man and a young boy try to get the dogs into the cage on the truck bed. Tiger goes right into the cage. The black one does not cooperate but doesn't run away. The two men are not friendly. We leave them battling with the black dog.

I bike only eleven miles but I'm tired, hungry, and worn out from the wind. Command Central calls it a day. We drive back to the Dancing Eagle Casino for lunch and try our luck at the slot machines. I love pulling the lever and watching the cherries, cloverleaves, dollar signs, and the many signs ding, ding, ding. Mostly I love hearing the clinging of quarters drop into the bucket when you win. We cash in at $36, $16 more than we started with, feeling rich and lucky.

We drive into Grants, which has necessities: a laundry, Wal-Mart, and a computer store. Jim's having problems with the connector cord on his computer, preventing AOL or wireless connection capabilities. No web page today but a motel room with a hot tub and pizza delivery. Tomorrow we will backtrack twenty miles and I'll bicycle into Grants.

> Red rocks climb the sky.
> Gray clouds kiss grazing sheep while
> White "Sky City" sleeps.

This geographically and historically diverse land includes dinosaur diggings, volcanoes, lava flows, desert, high rugged mountains and deep valleys. Despite the cold, the wind, and the raindrops, I can't take my eyes off the view. I have seen this country only in pictures and movies, so it looks familiar yet foreign. I have difficulty estimating distance. Sometimes the rocks are white mixed with the low clouds, and then they turn red, then black.

I have the road to myself. The only sounds I hear are birds and sometimes in the distance I hear a train whistle that brings me out of my reverie. I stop to take a picture of the cliff on my right. The red rocks look like a deserted village hanging over the cliff. How odd or am I seeing things? I'm alone for long periods of time, so it's possible.

Another cloudy-looks-like-rain-day. I want to get as many miles in before heavy rain starts. Just outside Grant and over the bridge is Milan, a town with a familiar name, though this Milan looks nothing like Milan, Ohio, where my grandfather, my mother, and Thomas A. Edison were born. That one is a charming little village with a town square that hasn't changed in one hundred years. This one is a strip of run down businesses that look like they could close any day. Before I have any more time to think, the town is gone.

I stop at a convenient store and find some postcards. One describes the Acoma Pueblo just a few miles east of Grant, the village hanging over the cliff that I had seen yesterday. The "Sky City" is built on a sandstone butte rising four hundred feet from the surrounding plain and is believed to be the oldest inhabited city in the U.S., built around the twelfth century. The name comes from the Keresan Indian words ako (white rock) and ma (people). The Spanish mission, Church of San Estevan de Ray dates to 1629-41. I wasn't seeing things.

I bike this double-lane, wide-bermed, somewhat flat road praying the rain will hold off until the end of the day. The sun peeks out but clouds dominate the sky. I reach the town of Prewitt, four worn-down houses, an old brick building, and the post office. I wonder if they will let me use their bathroom. I walk in and explain my situation. "I know that a post office does not have public facilities, but can you make an exception?

Yes, they can.

> "Rain, rain go away,"
> Sun, sun come out to play. Bring
> Glorious rainbow

The sun disappears for good but I keep riding. The red cliffs on one side of me and the railroad tracks on the other keep me company. It's getting colder but I want to go as far as I can before it rains. I ride through Thoreau, another familiar name. I stop to take a picture of a gas-station-store-restaurant with a sign painted on the front stating the elevation--7200 feet. After I bike seven miles, the road ends and it begins to rain, then to pour. Jim picks me up before I'm soaked. We see an Indian Village gift shop and a sign that reads:

Continental Divide- 7,275 ft. Rainfall divides at this point; to the west it drains into the Pacific Ocean; to the east it drains into the Atlantic Ocean.

And it's raining! We drive through Gallup to see it. As you might imagine, it's an old-fashioned cowboy town with the railroad tracks running straight through it. We stop at the El Rancho Hotel & Motel for lunch. The décor is Spanish/Indian with rustic wood beams, wood floors covered with woven Indian rugs, wagon-wheel chandeliers, and elk and deer heads mounted on the walls. A circular stairway in the giant lobby leads to the second-floor picture gallery of autographed photos of stars. Famous guests stayed here while filming the popular western movies: Ronald Reagan, Jane Wyman, Spencer Tracy, Katherine Hepburn, Kirk Douglas, and many others. Some have suites named for them. We look at the president's suite, Ronald Reagan, and decide it's out of our price range and no dogs are allowed.

It's raining hard. We have food, a hot tub, and wine. We are in heaven. We've traveled 405 miles from Amarillo to Gallup and are about 270 miles from Phoenix. I biked/walked 214 miles which means we drove 191 miles. We did more driving on this leg than the first two because the road we traveled often just stopped. The only other road through this country is Interstate Rt. 40, which prohibits pedestrians and bicycles. I have to average twenty-five miles a day to make it to Phoenix by our target date, November 21. That is if there is a road all the way and we don't have to stop for rain.

Another cloudy, cold day. We drive the twenty miles back to where we ended yesterday. A busy road and little berm but the wind comes from the east and pushes me along. I bike eight miles before it starts to pour. Again Jim gets to me before the rain. As we drive back to the hotel, a giant, clear, full rainbow arcs high in the sky, sun shining and rain pouring. This glorious sight reminds us of our purpose--the end of our journey is near.

Time to find a Radio Shack to buy a computer connector. The one we had repaired in Grants broke again. They didn't have the right kind but he directed us to a computer store that might be able to fix it. They can but Jim will have to leave his computer, which means no map program to guide our way.

The sun comes out. It's cold and sprinkling, but I don't mind. I ride through mud puddles alongside of the road. Mud splatters my pants and coat and I feel like a little girl playing out in the rain. What fun! It's cool and windy and looks like it will rain again but never does. Because Jim doesn't have his computer and map program, we miss a turn and go out of our way about a mile. He stops a policeman, the only other vehicle we have seen for miles, and asks for directions. The policeman points us in the right direction and back to the road we should have taken.

I look up at the rock formations and cliffs surrounding me. Ahead is the Arizona sun. I cry, thinking about how far I've come. Not just in miles but on my grief journey. I want to work more with suicide prevention and education. I want to speak and write and listen to others' stories. I want to help end suicide. I want to help others choose to live. I want to write a book about this journey to share with the world.

Chapter Twenty

Why Walk When You Can Fly

Here, Arizona,
Almost my long journey's end--
What do I do next?

I'm not paying attention to the road until I see a mile marker: State Line--10 miles, 9 miles, 8, 7, and finally 1 mile to the Arizona State Line. Another sign invites me to stop at "Wild Buffalo, Oldest Stop on Rt. 66" and then the Arizona State Line. I cross into Arizona but still don't believe it. Jim catches up and takes my picture standing in front of the Arizona State Line, the sun shining behind me. Back in Gallup we celebrate with dinner at a fancy restaurant and our weekly expedition to Wal-Mart. One more week and 247 miles to go.

We are anxious to start early on this sunny day, cool and glorious. It's my first day in the last state I will bike. We drive to the Arizona state line where I peddle off on a road that is all mine most of the day. With the exception of a couple of miles where the road doesn't exist, I bike all the way to the Petrified Forest and Painted Desert. I arrive there around 2:30, without enough time to ride through the 28-mile park before dark. We decide to take our time and go as far as I can and then complete it tomorrow. We want to take our time to appreciate its beauty and learn more about this mysterious place.

Jim stops at each scenic outlook and waits for me. We take time to soak in the beauty and then we continue. Because it's a National Park, the speed limit is 35 and is lightly trafficked this time of year and day. I take my time biking through the gently rolling hills of this heaven on earth. We spend some time at the visitor's center and tell them I'm biking through the park, which many people do. We did not realize that the Petrified Forest and the Painted Desert are parts of the same park. I remembered reading about it in school, never understanding how a forest of trees became stone so I had always wanted to see it. Now I am biking through it. Because we arrived here in the middle of the afternoon I can only bike half way before the park closes. Another thirty-five miles today and I am tired.

> Red, white, black sandstone,
> Blues, purples, grays, minerals,
> Ancient forest lives.

When we drive back to the park the next morning, the day is sunny and a comfortable temperature. We take our time driving to the halfway mark where we ended yesterday, stopping often to see the views in the morning light, which paints the scene quite differently from how the afternoon light did.

A raven starts following us. It appears to want food, but we have nothing to share. First, it flies close to us on the right, then on the left, then in front of us. He stays with us until he spots another car and heads their way. I hope they have food for him. Again I bike from one scenic point to the next where Jim waits for me. Some of the restrooms are closed which makes the distance between the open ones far apart. I ask Jim to find a hidden place where I can pee by the car.

The forest in the Petrified Forest does not exist today. However, 225 million years ago stately pine-like trees grew in this headwaters area. As they fell into the floodplain, silt, mud, and volcanic ash covered the logs. Silica-laden ground water seeped through the oxygen depleted logs and replaced the wood with silica deposits. Over the centuries, the silica crystallized into quartz and the logs were preserved as petrified wood. I did not understand this process until I stood on a cliff and looked out at the stone-like logs blanketing this lonesome land.

This land, this desert is foreign territory, a place I've never been before and do not wish to stay too long. The desert is where my son ended his life. In *Desert Solitaire*, Edward Abby says the desert is clear, simple, mysterious, motionless and silent. It does nothing but waits—and what it's waiting for is unknown. Was it waiting for a young man to make his final decision? I can't think about this anymore. I need, want to be in the NOW.

I am tempted to pick up a piece of petrified wood but obey the signs, "Do not pick up petrified wood." The park brochure repeats this plea. "Multiplied by hundreds of thousands of visitors per year, the small pieces stolen from the park can quickly amount to tons." Visitors are encouraged to purchase pieces from gift shops that sell deposits collected outside the park.

I finish the thirteen-mile ride and we head for Snowflake, where we eat lunch. Outside Snowflake, I hop on my bike and head for Show Low. I ride for two miles before giving up. The road is heavily trafficked and has no berm. The speed limit is 65, but cars and trucks are flying by at 70-75 mph, making me nervous and scared. I don't want to have an accident so close to the end of my trip. We drive through the White Mountains and into Show Low, advertised as, "Arizona's Four Season Location." We find the Best Western and check in. Jim drives me back to the edge of town where the sidewalk starts. I take a leisurely walk through town to the hotel, which is exactly two miles. Only seventeen miles today but it's time to rest.

We're in the mountains, making this morning colder. It's cloudy and windy, too. I begin riding right across the street where I finished walking yesterday. Again for one moment, I ask myself "What am I doing?" And again I remember. I continue focusing on the giant pine trees that remind me of North Carolina. And the smell, the smell is heavenly.

I follow the road, up and up and down and down. I pass the destruction made by the forest fires from a couple of years ago. I remember flying over them on our way to Phoenix. Before seeing the fire out the plane window, I smelled the smoke and became frightened. Then I saw the fire and smoke on the ground below. Now I see the destruction that remains.

I pass five to six descansos with two crosses in more than one location. These shrines to accident victims help me concentrate on this deadly road more carefully. I do not want my name on a cross at the side of this road! I see a couple riding a Harley, which makes me think of Dick. I spoke with him yesterday. He'll be meeting us on Friday for the ceremony I have planned at the spot where Eric ended his life. I haven't finalized the details but wherever and whenever, Dick will be there to meet us.

I walk the bike several times today, as the hills are becoming small mountains. Sometimes I feel like I'm flying down the mountain. I know I'm going too fast but I want to FLY! I add verses to my chant:

Miles of forest yesterday,
Red rock hills today.
Giant pines that kiss the moon.
My glorious journey ending soon.
I thank You, I thank You,
Namaste, I thank You.

Only twenty-five miles today but I'm tired. Since we've been in the mountains, we've had no signal for the Internet and are not able to publish web pages or get e-mails. We feel out of touch with the world. Soon we will be in Phoenix; soon we will be celebrating the end of this journey. Soon I will be able to rest. But tomorrow, I'll be back on the bike. Tonight, fresh-baked chocolate-chip cookies in the motel lobby, laundry, dinner, and a trip to K-mart, no Wal-Mart here.

We eat dinner at the Mesa, an Italian restaurant that sounds Mexican. A young couple with a tiny baby sits at the next table. We tell them,"Your baby is beautiful." Alex and Donna share their story. "Three weeks ago we drove from San Diego to Colorado to be with the birth mother when she went into labor. We were with her throughout the entire labor and birth of the baby. Donna even cut the cord. We named her after Donna's aunt, Juliet." We wished them a wonderful life with their new daughter.

It's a blessing to meet a new mother embodying all the wonder, possibilities, and dreams of the future, of life itself. Other mothers I've met along this journey have been struggling with the realities of sorrow and grief. Karen, whose son attempted suicide and failed, leaving him emotionally and physically scarred. Laurie, estranged from her daughter, fears for her daughter's future. Tracy's daughter died too young. The Madonna of the Trail stone statures, representing pioneer mothers who struggled and followed their men into an unknown land, into an unknown future. And the fictional "Ma" in John Steinbeck's, *The Grapes of Wrath,* whose strength and determination kept the Joad family together as they traveled this same road I now travel. All the mothers who have lost a son or a daughter, women who keep going because that's all we can do. And all we can do is pray that we will someday recover our wonder, our sense of possibility, in a future time when we learn to fully live again on down the road.

This is our last week on the road. We'll be in Phoenix by the end of the week. But now I have to get through the mountains. Another cold and windy day of biking when the road has a berm, driving when it disappears, biking, driving, on and on. The mountains, the canyons and the tall pines make it difficult to believe we are in Arizona. I just know Phoenix, Sedona, and the Grand Canyon. This is not that same Arizona. Again I fly down and down to what I thought was the bottom of the Salt River Canyon. But I'm only half-way. The berm ends and the road begins to twist and turn and curve down the mountainside. Time to end my bike ride, too dangerous.

We walk down the boardwalk to the river where venders sell homemade jewelry. We stare at the view as we cross the river and head up the mountain. I am not biking here. We stop a couple of times at scenic overlooks. We see a woman taking pictures; we pull out our camera and ask, "Will you take our picture?" Then, "Where are you from?"

"My mother and I are from Germany and we're visiting friends here in Arizona."

"We visited your country several times and love it." I show her my walking stick with emblems from several cities in Germany.

"Where are you from?" she asks.

When we tell her what we are doing and why, she begins to cry.

"I can't imagine that. I miss my sons but I will be seeing them soon when we get home." We hug and wish each other safe journeys.

> Memories of Eric
> Seep into my mind. How do
> I tell his story?

Today I walk through downtown Globe, Claypool, and Miami, Arizona. These old mining towns run together and I like being in civilization for a change. The altitude is getting to me. Jim feels it, too. Angela, the reporter from the *Arizona*

Republic called. She wants to interview me in person and take some pictures.

We arrive in Superior just in time for lunch and find a quaint Mexican restaurant, the only restaurant in town. After lunch we have time to waste before meeting Angela. We drive down Main Street and find an antique store that looks as antique as the town. I see a tray of small black stones with one tiny white spot on each. The owner shares the story of the Apache Tears.

"The mountain overlooking the town is called Apache Leap. In 1870, white settlers forced a small tribe of Apaches up the mountain and surrounded them. Instead of surrendering, they all leapt to their deaths. These stones found at the bottom of the mountain have their tears to remind us of the story."

I finger the stones in the tray, sensing the tears of so many lives lost then and now. We tell her that I'm walking and biking because my son chose to end his life.

She places a stone in my hand for my son.

We meet Angela back at the restaurant. She interviews us for over an hour, asking the same questions she asked on the phone: what was Eric's childhood like, what kind of boy/man was he and why did he take his own life? I've asked and answered these questions these past ten years. And when I hear her last question, "Why did he take his own life?" I no longer need to ask why. I need only to continue on; healing, loving, and living each moment, this moment.

Angela asks, "Did you see the shrine to miners back in Miami when you came through?"

"No, we did not."

"I'd like to show it to you. I think you'll find it appropriate for what you are doing."

We drive back to Miami and find the shrine. It is filled with pictures, flowers, candles, letters, and poems in memory of all the miners who have died in the mines around here. I leave one of my key chains. Angela says, "Your story will be in Friday's paper, Eric's birthday."

Earlier when I walked through Miami, I passed a bookstore. It is open now and we stop. While I look for books, Jim visits with the owner, Maureen. "What's the best place in town to have dinner?"

"The Driftwood Inn has the juiciest hamburgers in town, and I'll be there later. Please stop by."

We had passed the seedy-looking place the night before. It looks like a dive but we take her recommendation. It is dark and quaint and full of locals, just what we like. We sit at the bar and talk to the men on each side of us. Jim talks to Doug and I to John. Both are from the Globe area. There's Maureen: "How do you like this place?"

"You're right about the hamburgers. They're juicy and delicious, better than we expected." This place gloomy looking on the outside is a charming, and welcoming bar on the inside. John listens to our story and wants to hear all the details. We give him our website. When the bartender hands us our bill, John takes it. "I want to buy your dinner to give to your cause." Thank you, John.

Today is my last day. My last day of the journey, my last day to bike, my last day to walk, my last mile. I wonder what will it be like?

First I notice it's warmer. I don't need my jacket or gloves, just my t-shirt and short pants. It's sunny but windy. For a while I bike several easy miles, the wind pushing me along. Then I change directions and I'm riding into the wind again, moving slowly. It's difficult but that doesn't last long.

When I reach Rt. 79, the wind is at my back again and I sail along the straight, lightly traveled road. I reach Arizona Farm Road. Again this does not look like Arizona because dairy and cattle farms and cotton fields border this road. Next to the cotton fields, train-car size cotton bales line the road. All I can think about is that I am coming to the end. I know Jim is probably thinking this, too. I plan to ride down

Hunt Highway to about five miles from Lindsey Road, which is the approximate location where Eric ended his life. When I reach Hunt Highway, the dirt road of eleven years ago is a busy road with new housing developments, shopping centers, churches, schools, and a library, with new streets intersecting it. Most are not even on the map. I cannot believe it! But just as I have changed in these last eleven years, this area has also changed. It is allowed to change—just as I am allowed to. Then the road ends and my journey ends!

We drive around looking at the new golf communities. This lonely desert my son drove out into to be alone to write a suicide note and then shoot himself is now filled with houses, condos, stores, schools, and streets going in every direction. It is filled with life! We find Lindsey Road and then the intersection with Hunt Highway, which is closed for construction. But we can walk to it. We will have Eric's birthday celebration at that spot on Friday. I will think about that tomorrow. Today we celebrate with my daughter and son-in-law and my three grandchildren.

Journal Entry
November 21, 2003

Dear Eric,

How do I begin to tell you about today, your 31ˢᵗ birthday? Because we arrived two days earlier than planned, we had a day of much-needed rest. As soon as we arrived and after hugging and kissing the kids, we heard the cling-clang of an ice cream truck. We hurried outside to buy treats, laughing and crying.

In addition to the article for The Arizona Republic, *the NBC television station, owned by the same company, called and asked if I could be interviewed for the local early morning show. Tomorrow is National Survivor of Suicide Day sponsored by the American Foundation for Suicide*

Prevention. Since 1998, AFSP has sponsored a teleconference consisting of a panel of survivors who answer questions for other survivors.

Local organizations televise the conference and provide local information about survivor groups. Before we left for this last phase I contacted the local group here in Phoenix to tell them about my journey and say that I would be attending tomorrow as an appropriate ending to this pilgrimage. They asked me to speak and share my story. I will share this information with viewers in my interview.

Jim, Laura and I awoke at 4:30 am to arrive at the station downtown by 5:30. I was so excited I couldn't sleep late anyway. The interview seemed to fly, we were in and out of the station in what seemed like minutes. They gave me a copy of the interview. I look like a little girl, not a fifty - something woman who just biked across the country.

On the way home we stopped for a paper. On the first page of the local section was our story. "Mom on a healing journey, Trekking across country to raise suicide awareness." Angela wrote a moving and informational story. She shared stories about you and about my healing and walk/bike journey. She included the warning signs of suicide and where to get help locally. She had quotes from our web page and a map showing our entire route.

After reading the article and crying, we all packed into the car and drove the 45 minutes south back to Hunt Highway and Lindsay Road. Our friends Sue, Reed, and Dick all on their Harleys met us for our ending ceremony. The kids and I made you another desconsos yesterday. They wrote you notes saying they love you and miss you. Alec's says, "You're a bad boy with the tattoo thing." I read a poem from Giving Sorrow Words.

For My Young Friends Who Are Afraid

There is a country to cross you will
find in the corner of your eye, in
the quick slip of your foot-air far
down, a snap that might have caught.
And maybe for you, for me, a high, passing
voice that finds its way by being
afraid. That country is there, for us,
carried as it is crossed. What you fear
will not go away: it will take you into
yourself and bless you and keep you.
That's the world and we all live there.

--William Stafford

We shared our thoughts and feelings and celebrated you and me and our healing journey. Then I hopped on the back of Dick's Harley and drove down that busy highway back into our present lives. As I wrapped my arms tightly around Dick's waist, tears streamed down my cheeks, tears of joy, happiness, healing, and love. This is the last time I visit this place of death. I don't need to come here anymore.

No clouds, just blue sky
and warm, bright sun welcomes me
to my journey's end.

Chapter Twenty-one

Suddenly I See

January 7, 2004

Dear Eric,

On this day I will always have the same thought when I wake up: This is the day you chose to die. Today is Thursday which it was eleven years ago when the policeman came to tell me you were dead. I don't know what I'm going to do today. Maybe drive to the cemetery, but so much snow covers the ground I probably wouldn't be able to find your grave.

I don't feel like doing anything. I usually don't on this day. I did put your baby photos in an album as I've wanted to do for years. I look at the pictures of you smiling, playing with Heidi, eating clams, acting silly. Where did that little boy go?

I got a call from a woman who got my name from Townhall II, which provides a 24 hour crisis hotline. She wanted to talk to someone who had experienced a loved one's suicide. Because of you, it's what I do now. Strange that she chose today to call me. I said, "My son died eleven years ago today and I still miss him."

A friend told her to call me.
She said I would understand.
I would listen. I would know.
She wanted to talk about her son
Not knowing that I wanted to talk about mine.
Two mothers sharing their stories,
Not of their son's lives but of their deaths.

One Monday afternoon, Michael took a shotgun
And walked across the road and into the woods.
She heard a shot but had no thought that her
Son chose to die that Monday afternoon in that woods.

He wrote a poem to say good-bye and
he would always love Jennifer.
Her grief still fresh, she asks God, why, why, why
Did my son choose to die?

One Thursday morning, Eric took a handgun
And drove down the road and into the desert.
He wrote a note to say good-bye and
He would always love Beth.
My grief is older but it surfaces today, his death day.
I no longer ask why, just try to get through the day.
Funny she should call today.
Two mothers sharing their stories of sons
Who chose to die.

Today Helen sent me an E-mail with notes from the Deena Metzger workshop at the *Common Boundary* conference we attended in 1993. "When creativity and spirituality meet it is a VISION. Write six titles of the books you want to write before you die. Then write the first paragraph. Then write the first page. To get the answer to a spiritual question: write the question, write the story of an ordinary event, the answer to the question is in the story."

Today I begin to write our story about the past and also begin to live my future.

Epilogue

Holding the Lifekeeper bracelet that my friend Sandy designed after her son's suicide. I retrace the infinity sign, the number eight. It was eight years after Eric died that I walked the marathon and for the first time felt healthy and whole. And now it has taken me eight years to write our story. Eight years of reading my journals and transcribing them into my computer, of remembering the pain and joy of Eric's life and death, of writing our story and making sense of my life, then and now. Eight years of life going on while learning how to live again. Another eight-year journey in writing, one of achievement, accomplishment, and fulfillment, and now completion.

The number eight is significant to Scorpio, Eric's astrological sign because it represents deep change and transformation. I know I have changed and I believe Eric has also. I believe whereever he is, he is now at peace with his life, his death, and himself.

We were on the road over eighty days and traveled over 1,800 miles through eight states: Ohio, Indiana, Illinois, Missouri, Oklahoma, Texas, New Mexico, and Arizona. In my training and the journey to follow, I wore out eight pairs of shoes. If I counted, I'm sure my bike went through eight inner tubes.

I experienced and learned about the eight aspects of suicide grief: shock and denial, guilt, depression, anger, resentment, relief, abandonment and isolation.

In these past eight years, eight family members and close friends have died: Jim's father and stepmother; our dear friends Sara, Sandy, Leslie, Mike, Roger and Frieda. I regret that they did not have the opportunity to read this story in which all played significant parts.

I memorized my favorite Biblical verse, *Ecclesiates* 3:1-8.

To everything there is a season, and a time to every purpose under heaven:
a time to be born and a time to die; a time to plant and a time to uproot,
a time to kill and a time to heal, a time to tear down and a time to build,
a time to weep and a time to laugh, a time to mourn and a time to dance,
a time to scatter stones and a time to gather them, a time to embrace and a time to refrain,
a time to search and a time to give up, a time to keep and a time to throw away,
a time to tear and a time to mend, a time to be silent and a time to speak,
a time to love and a time to hate, a time for war and a time for peace.

And now a time to celebrate and live.

Afterword

To those who have lost a loved one to suicide and traveled this journey with me, I hope that my story has helped you in your healing journey. Even though it's been eighteen years since Eric took his life, I still think of him every day. I remember those first few days and months after his death when I wondered if I would get through this, yet here I am living a full, healthy, joyful, and love-filled life.

Jim and I travel to visit our kids and grandkids in Phoenix, Tampa, and Austin. We spend time at our second home in Southern Pines, N.C., where I wrote most of this book. We've traveled with friends and family to Europe several times since 1993, including one trip to Spain to re-trace the steps of my life there in 1969. This year we're planning a trip to Germany to visit my sister and her family. And in November we're returning to Phoenix for an exciting celebration. After attending the University of Phoenix for three years, my daughter Laura will receive her Bachelor of Business Administration degree. We are so proud of her and would not miss this occasion.

I walk many miles a week alone and with my friend Anne, ride my bike, and get to yoga class as often as I can. I am active in my local American Legion Post 803 and enjoy marching in our Memorial Day and Independence Day parades.

In the past eight years, my mother and I have established a relationship we never had before. I am thankful that she lived long enough and that I was able to learn to express gratitude and forgiveness so we could enjoy a real mother-daughter relationship. Perhaps my next healing story will be about that journey.

Last year we created the Eric Llewellyn Fund affiliated with the Coleman Foundation that provides funds for Coleman Professional Services, a mental-health agency. A portion of the proceeds from this book will be donated to that fund for suicide education and prevention. I co-facilitate a Survivor of Suicide support group in my community and am active on our county suicide-prevention coalition. I share my story with civic organizations, schools and churches. With this book, I hope to expand the reach of my story to other communities.

I still write letters to Eric on his birthday and on the anniversary of his death. I continue to journal. Two years ago I trained as a facilitator for a journal-writing program, *Journal to the Self,* by Kay Adams. I want to help others learn the power of journaling.

However, I still experience remnants of grief. Last October I attended my nephew Aric's wedding. I sat with my mother who smiled through the entire ceremony. We enjoyed watching the bride and groom cut the wedding cake and dance as husband and wife. When Aric danced with his mother, though, I ran from the room, crying. Jim found me and held me in his arms until the dance ended. The fact that I will never dance at my son's wedding is a loss that is always with me.

But Eric continues to help me, too. A few months before completing this book, my ex-husband and I discovered we had purchased a life insurance policy on Eric when he was a year old. We had lost the paper work and forgot about it until the insurance company contacted us, eighteen years after his death. So Eric sent us this money at the time I needed it to self-publish our story. I know he will be with me, guiding me until I see him one sweet day.

I pray that one day your life will be filled with strength, health, joy, and gratitude as you continue on your healing journey. When I look back on my own eighteen years without Eric, I see that my losses and gains are so closely woven that they form a tapestry, a rich, many-hued carpet that I can walk on fearlessly, and with gratitude for what is given and what remains.

Iris Llewellyn Angle

June 19, 2011

Grace and Gratitude

Meister Eckhart said, "If the only prayer you ever said in your whole life was "thank you" that would suffice."

This is my "thank you" prayer.

To God for bringing me out of the well of grief and into the sunshine to thrive and live a full life.

To my husband, Jim who I fell in love with because he made me laugh. He held me when I cried, patiently let me grieve in my own way and time, lead the way as we traveled across the country and helped me learn to laugh again.

To my son, Eric who gave us love and laughter and taught me compassion, empathy, how to make a difference in my world and how to really live.

To my daughter, Laura who taught me love, patience, friendship, companionship, wisdom, and great joy.

To my seven grandchildren; Alec, Cameron, Sierra, Jimmy, Joey, Jon, and Hadley who give me much joy and reminds me that life does go on.

To my mother, Violet Wagner who taught me understanding, forgiveness, forgetfulness, compassion and finally love.

To Eric's friends who are still in my life; Beth Stein

Kotowski, Tabitha Desz, Gabe Barrett, and those I
haven't seen in a while but I know they still think of
him.

To Rose Radank, my sister, my brother-in-law, John
and my nephew, Bobby who took care of us that first
week of Eric's death. And for sharing and understanding
what I was going through. And thank you, Rose for
your letter I shared in my story.

To my friends who traveled this journey with me and
still love me:

Diane-Worthington Garey who taught me to grieve
with dignity and to go on living and loving life.

Elizabeth Norris for her encouragement and
wisdom.

Shannon Mihal who cried and laughed with me and
reminded me of how strong I am and to her children,
Amber and Aric who are my godchildren.

Dick Wactler, who first took me to where Eric
ended his life, was there when I finished my
pilgrimage and has been there for me in all the
years between.

Roger Arbaugh who sent me daily encouraging
e-mails to keep me going on my pilgrimage. I am
thankful I shared my first draft with him before he
died.

Janet Douglass who was my witness that first week
of grief, for her letter and her children, Leah and
Galen, my godchildren.

Helen Sadler, my teacher who encouraged me to grow, learn, pray, and become a writer. I lost count of how many drafts of my book she read and gave me suggestions for improving it. After reading one of my drafts she made a CD of songs she heard in her head as she read. The songs are the chapter titles.

Anne Albanese, my walking partner and listener. We've walked and talked a million miles and continue today.

To my cheerleaders who continuously encouraged me to keep writing: Helen Sadler, Anne Albanese, Linda Harvey, and Sue Dallman.

To those who gave me hope in the dark hours of my early grief, who encouraged me to heal and stretch my abilities: my sister, Rose Radank, my brother, Ed Wagner, my friends; Diane-Worthington Garey, Shannon Mihal, Janet Douglass, Helen Sadler, Karen Leland, Cecelia Jaskolski, Julie Mitchell, Nancy Allen, Beverly "Chris" High, Elizabeth Norris, Carol Stoner, Rev. Kevin Horak, Rev. Everette Chapman, Rev. Ben McGee, Iris Bolton, Sandy Martin, Amie Cajka, Ruth Simera, my Toastmaster's group and all the survivors I met in the survivor of suicide community.

To Zachery Voelker and all the members of the Team-In-Training from the Leukemia and Lymphoma Society.

To Dr. Tony Badalamenti my chiropractor for his exercise programs to help me get into shape.

To those who walked with me for a while on my physical journey: Jim and Betsy Anderson, Susan Duppstadt and Roger Sparhawk, Beth Stein Kotowski, Tabitha Desz, Gabe and Jordon Barrett, John Shannon, Amy Davidson and her daughters; Heather, Caitlin and Mikayla, Anne Albannese, Pam Richards, Janet and Leah Douglass.

To our friends who we stayed with in St. Louis, Mary Kay, David and Sarah Crawford.

To our friends Sue and Reed Dallman who met us in Albuquerque when we traveled through New Mexico.

To all the people we met on our pilgrimage who shared their stories and encouraged us to complete the journey.

To those who were there at the end and celebrated our journey's end, a new beginning and Eric's life: my daughter and her family, Dick Wactler, Sue and Reed Dallman.

To those who helped me become a better writer:

Helen Sadler who read all my drafts and made it better.

Marsha McGregor who gave me suggestions for improving my book and permission to share her poem, "To Iris."

Lou Suarez who thought my poem, "Night Sky" worthy of first place in a poetry contest.

David Hassler who taught me to teach poetry in his class, "Teaching Poetry in the Schools at Kent State University.

Carole Richards for giving me the opportunity to teach poetry at her kids camp.

John Kusik for introducing me to the Serenity Prayer.

Dr. Joel Mowery and Dr. Jack Jordan who
suggested that I write the Afterward.

Kay Adams for leading me to become a facilitator for
"Journal to the Self."

John Fox for introducing me to poetry therapy and the
National Association for Poetry Therapy.

Deanna R. Adams for her supports, knowledge and
directing the Lakeland Community College Writing
Conference where I learned about writing and publishing.

All the authors I've read and met over the years who
graciously shared their talents and wisdom.

To Angela Cara Pancrazio the reporter who shared my story
in the Arizona Republic.

To Nelson Burns, Bill Childers and all my dedicated friends
at Coleman Foundation who helped us create the Eric
Llewellyn Fund for Suicide Prevention and Education.

To Linda Hobson, my editor who worked diligently to make
my book "the best it could be."

To my three dogs; Heidi, Kitty and Biscuit who taught me to
become a dog person and a better person for it.

I could not have succeeded on this grief journey, the physical
journey or the writing of this book journey
without your love, support, and encouragement.

Thank you and Namaste.

Permissions

Cousineau, Phil. *The Art of Pilgrimage; The Seeker's Guide to Making Travel Sacred.* Copyright 1998 Phil Cousineau. www.tedwheelweiser.com, 1-800-423-7087.

Estes, Clarissa Pinkola, Ph.D. Quotes on pages 44 and 125 are excerpted from *Women Who Run with the Wolves* with kind permission of publisher and author Dr. Clarissa Pinkola Estes, Copyright 1996 all rights reserved.

Mazza, Nicholas. "Hope." *The Journal of Humanities Education and Development, 36,257.*

Stafford, William. "For My Friends Who Are Afraid" and "Yes" from *The Way It Is: New and Selected Poems.* Copyright 1976, 1991 by William Stafford and the Estate of William Stafford. Reprinted with permission of Graywolf Press, Minneapolis, Minnesota, www.graywolf.org.

Wolfelt, Dr. Alan. *Journey Through Grief, Reflections on Healing.* www.centerforloss.com.

Works Cited

Apollinaire, Guillaume. "Come to the Edge."

Abby, Edward. *Desert Solitaire, A Season in the Wilderness.* Ballantine Books, 1985.

Adams, Kay. *Journal to the Self.* Warner Books Inc. 1990.

Basho, Matsao.

The Bible. Ecclesiastes 3:1-8

Bolton, Iris. *My Son, My Son.* Bolton Press Atlanta, 1983.

Borysenko, Joan.

Confucius.

Cousineau, Phil. *The Art of Pilgrimage; The Seeker's Guide to Making Travel Sacred.* Weiser Books, 1998.

Covey, Stephen. *The 7 Habits of Highly Effective People.* Simon and Schuster, 1989.

Emerson, Ralph Waldo.

Estes, Clarissa Pincola, Ph.D. *Women Who Run With Wolves.* Ballantine Books, 1992.

Frankl, Victor. *Man's Search for Meaning.* Pocket Books, 1959, 1962, 1984.

Gawain, Shakti. *The Path of Transformation; How Healing Ourselves Can Heal the World.* Natarja Publishing, 1993.

Gibran, Kahil. *The Prophet.*

Guiley, Rosemary Ellen. *Angels of Mercy. Pocket Books, 1994.*

Hamilton, Robert Brown. "Untitled Poem."

Hanh, Tchich Nhat. *Being Peace.* Parrallax Press. 1987.

Judd, Naomi. *Love Can Build a Bridge,* Fawcett Crest, 1993.

MacLaine, Shirley. *The Camino, A Journey of the Sprit.* Pocket Books, 2000.

Mazza, Nicholas. "Hope." *The Journal of Humanistic Education and Development,* 1998.

McGregor, Marsha. "For Iris."

Metzger, Deena. *Writing for Your Life.* Harper Collins Publisher. 1992.

Mother Teresa.

National Association of Poetry Therapy, *Giving Sorrow Words, Poems of Strength and Solace.* 2002.

Neibuhr, Reinhold. "Serenity Prayer."

Oliver, Mary. "The Journey." *Dream Work.* Atlantic Monthly Press, 1986.

Rilke, Rainer Marie. *Letters to a Poet.*

St. Francis of Assissi. "Instrument of Peace."

Stafford, William. "For My Friends Who Are Afraid" and "Yes" from *The Way It Is: New and Selected Poems.* Copyright 1976, 1991. Graywolf Press.

Talan, Deb. Song "Tell Your Story Walking."

Thomas, Marlo. *The Right Words at the Right Time.* Atria Books, 2002.

Thoreau, Henry David. *Walking.*

Tole, Eckhart. *The Power of Now.* Namaste Publishing, 1999.

Walsh, Neale Donald. *Conversation with God, Book 3.* Hampton Road Publishing Company, Inc. 1998.

Whitman, Walt. "Song of Myself."

Wolfelt, Dr. Alan. Journey *Through Grief, Reflections on Healing.*

About the Author

Iris Llewellyn Angle's healing journey changed her life in ways she could never imagine. She co-facilitates a survivor of suicide group in Kent, Ohio and is a member of the Portage County Suicide Prevention Coalition. She participates in the local American Foundation for Suicide Prevention teleconference on National Survivor of Suicide Day, the Saturday before Thanksgiving. She presents speeches on suicide and grief to organizations, churches, and schools. She is a trained facilitator for "Journal to the Self" and teaches journal writing and poetry. She volunteers for the Coleman Foundation to raise funds for Coleman Professional Services.

Iris continues to walk, bike, practice yoga, journal and write and teaches poetry. She, her husband Jim, and their dog Biscuit enjoy traveling the country and the world to visit family and friends.

Made in the USA
Columbia, SC
27 December 2020

27268919R20143